ROUTLEDGE LIBRARY EDITIONS:
URBAN AND REGIONAL ECONOMICS

Volume 17

REGIONAL ECONOMIC
DEVELOPMENT AND POLICY

REGIONAL ECONOMIC DEVELOPMENT AND POLICY
Theory and Practice in the European Community

DAVID PINDER

Routledge
Taylor & Francis Group

LONDON AND NEW YORK

First published in 1983 by Allen & Unwin

This edition first published in 2018
by Routledge
2 Park Square, Milton Park, Abingdon, Oxon OX14 4RN

and by Routledge
711 Third Avenue, New York, NY 10017

Routledge is an imprint of the Taylor & Francis Group, an informa business

British Library Cataloguing in Publication Data
A catalogue record for this book is available from the British Library

ISBN: 978-1-138-09590-8 (Set)
ISBN: 978-1-315-10306-8 (Set) (ebk)
ISBN: 978-1-138-10198-2 (Volume 17) (hbk)
ISBN: 978-1-315-10314-3 (Volume 17) (ebk)

Publisher's Note
The publisher has gone to great lengths to ensure the quality of this reprint but points out that some imperfections in the original copies may be apparent.

Disclaimer
The publisher has made every effort to trace copyright holders and would welcome correspondence from those they have been unable to trace.

Regional Economic Development and Policy

Theory and Practice in the European Community

DAVID PINDER

Department of Geography, University of Southampton

University Association for Contemporary European Studies

George Allen & Unwin

George Allen & Unwin (Publishers) Ltd,
40 Museum Street, London WC1A 1LU, UK

George Allen & Unwin (Publishers) Ltd,
Park Lane, Hemel Hempstead, Herts HP2 4TE, UK

Allen & Unwin Inc.,
9 Winchester Terrace, Winchester, Mass 01890, USA

George Allen & Unwin Australia Pty Ltd,
8 Napier Street, North Sydney, NSW 2060, Australia

First published in 1983

Satellite picture of Europe reproduced courtesy of the Commission of the
European Communities

British Library Cataloguing in Publication Data

Pinder, David
    Regional economic development and policy.— (Studies
    on contemporary Europe; no. 5)
    1. Regional planning—European Economic Community
    countries
    2. European Economic Community countries—Economic
    conditions
    I. Title   II. Series
    330.94   HC241.2

    ISBN 0-04-320152-0
    ISBN 0-04-320153-9 Pbk

Library of Congress Cataloging in Publication Data

Pinder, David
    Regional economic development and policy.
    (Studies in contemporary Europe; 5)
Bibliography: p.
Includes index.
1. European Economic Community countries—Economic
conditions—Regional disparities. 2. Regional planning
—European Economic Community countries. 3. European
Economic Community countries—Economic policy. I. Title.
II. Series: Studies in contemporary Europe (University
Association for Contemporary European Studies); 5.
HC241.2.P538 1983   338.94   82-21793

ISBN 0-04-320152-0
ISBN 0-04-320153-9 (pbk.)

Set in 11 on 12 point Plantin by Preface Ltd, Salisbury
and printed in Great Britain by Mackays of Chatham.

Contents

Editor's Preface

The University Association for Contemporary European Studies (UACES) exists to promote the study of contemporary European society in all its aspects. To do so it brings together a large number of scholars from many different disciplines. One motivating force for these scholars has been an awareness of the inadequacy of their particular scholarly discipline to provide satisfactory answers to the complex problems which they were handling both in research and in teaching. Many aspects of contemporary European economy, society and politics are indeed hard to illuminate if the light comes from only one of the traditional disciplines of academic study and this has meant that teachers, students and everybody else are frequently without adequate information on topics of immediate and important interest. The Association has therefore commissioned scholars currently working in such areas to present in short form studies of problems which are of special importance, or specially noteworthy because of the lack of easily accessible information about them in current public and academic discussion. The studies are written by experts in each particular topic. They are not, however, merely for teachers and students, but for anyone who may wish to find out something further about subjects which are now much discussed but about which real information is still hard to come by. In this way the Association hopes it may bring closer what are often the separate worlds of academic and public knowledge while at the same time providing a service to readers and students in a relatively new field of study.

ALAN S. MILWARD
*University of Manchester Institute
of Science and Technology*

Author's Preface

The literature relating to regional development in Europe is immense, and it cannot be claimed that this book represents an exhaustive survey of what is available. Instead it is based on a cross-section, selected to illustrate the multifaceted nature of regional systems, regional problems and interventionist policies. I am, of course, indebted to the many authors whose ideas and evidence are interwoven in the text. My gratitude must also be extended to many national and regional planners, especially those with whom I have had contact in the Netherlands and Belgium in the last decade. They have provided invaluable insights into the intricacies of regional economic systems. Also, in a period of increasing economic uncertainty, they have done nothing to conceal the many obstacles facing those attempting to strengthen regional economies through the implementation of planning strategies.

Nearer home my thanks are due to Mrs R. Flint, who typed the manuscript with her usual efficiency and skill, and to Miss J. Hoyle and Miss D. Marshallsay of Southampton University Library, who provided invaluable assistance in the exploration of the European Communities collection.

DAVID PINDER

1 *Origins*

Between the end of the Second World War and the oil crisis of 1973 the economies of Western Europe enjoyed a period of unprecedented growth. There were, of course, spatial and temporal variations in the rate of expansion, but a sharp contrast with prewar conditions was unmistakable at an early stage, and realisation of this change gave rise to optimism that the return of severe depression could be avoided. Although the resurrection of prosperity was founded on a wave of industrialisation, the initial power of which paradoxically owed much to the war's demands for rapid technological progress, the spirit of optimism was also based on a belief in the value of government intervention. Planning in many spheres now became the vogue, with management of the economy lying at the heart of the interventionist philosophy. The practice of economic management had several targets, the most important being the control of demand to iron out cyclical fluctuations, the promotion of industry in order to raise the aggregate level of national wealth and the application of regional policies in an attempt to distribute growth more evenly than the unfettered play of market forces would dictate. This book is concerned with the pursuit of the third of these goals in European Community countries and in the Community itself, but it is not intended to provide a detailed examination of development levels and planning measures throughout the Community's regions. Instead the focus is on broad issues and, in particular, on questions of theory and practice in regional economic planning.

Reasons for the emphasis on practice are largely self-evident; the design, application and impact of regional policies are obvious issues, although this does not diminish their importance. The need for a theorectical perspective is perhaps less clear, and it is certainly true that much of the literature, including Scargill's well-known series Problem Regions of Europe, does not emphasise this aspect of the subject. However, the argument for providing a theoretical foundation can be established with the aid of a medical analogy. Regional economic problems may be seen as symptoms of an illness, symptoms which we may attempt to treat by the application of regional policy. Yet a single symptom may arise from a variety of causes and, if diagnosis is to be successful, an understanding of the processes governing the functioning and malfunctioning of regional economic systems is essential. In later chapters, therefore, an examination of current theories and their relationships with Community regional problems precedes consideration of regional policies and their effects. Before we turn to theoretical issues, however, the remainder of this chapter will set theory and practice in context by outlining the historical background to regional economic planning in the Community and by describing the revolution in regional studies that has paralleled and contributed to the regional interventionist movement.

The Rise of Regional Policies

Thirlwall (1974) has pointed out that by the mid-1970s regional policies were normally justified by reference to three goals: the search for greater social justice, the strengthening or maintenance of political cohesion and the more efficient use of under-utilised national resources. Historically, the most catalytic of these was recognition of the need for social justice, a factor stemming from experience of the 1930s Depression. This cannot be considered at length, but there is ample literature and Aldcroft's (1978) work on the European economy in the twentieth century provides a good starting point for those wishing to investigate the subject further.

The fundamental significance of the Depression was that, especially in traditional industrial areas, unemployment and consequent poverty achieved a magnitude so great that political opinion, often in the form of new parties with socialist backgrounds, moved to support the view that a repetition should not be countenanced in countries or in regions. Genuine hope that a repetition could be avoided came from observation of the United States, where the New Deal experiment demonstrated the potential role that public expenditure could play in re-establishing growth. Although many politicians of the day would probably have been reluctant to admit it, it was also obvious that in Nazi Germany public expenditure, focusing first on infrastructure and then on rearmament, confirmed the conclusions that could be drawn from the New Deal. Yet, while some attempts to counteract the Depression were made in other European countries, most notably in Sweden where a very active public expenditure policy was pursued between 1931 and 1935, most governments remained unwilling to accept increasing budget deficits in return for reduced unemployment. Indeed, the common inclination was to curtail expenditure as part of general deflationary policies, a strategy that did not always spare the rudimentary social security systems then in existence. Consequently, it was not until the postwar period that full-employment policies linked to the concept of control via public expenditure finally emerged.

When they did so they were based not only on experience and observation of interwar developments, but also on the arguments advanced by Keynes (1936). His work, together with subsequent elaborations, strongly reinforced the view that governments had both the ability and the responsibility to counteract recessions. At the same time, however, it was feared that the achievement of sustained growth would in all probability work to the advantage of a small number of relatively favoured regions. After all, the prewar years were not devoid of new industrialisation, and much of the investment that had been made was biased away from traditional industrial areas. As a result, whereas Britain had ploughed a lonely furrow with its prewar Special Areas legislation (Pitfield, 1978), in the 1950s policies intended to take work to the workers became the norm. A detailed review of this development has been provided by Yuill, Allen and Hull (1980) and the general pattern is clear: Italy led the way in 1950 by establishing the *Cassa per il Mezzogiorno* and was rapidly followed by Germany (1951), the Netherlands (1951–2) and Ireland (1952). By the mid-1950s France had embarked on the same path, while the ranks were completed by Denmark (1958) and Belgium (1959).

Impressive though this movement may seem, in most cases the policies adopted were initially tentative with respect to designated areas and instruments, partly because the power of the forces to be overcome was not fully appreciated, and partly because the primary concern in the early postwar period remained the achievement of rapid national growth rates. But minor recessions in the early and late 1950s demonstrated that unemployment in poorly favoured regions could quickly rise as the strength of expansionary forces weakened. Given the prevailing commitment to full employment, this continuing imbalance in the labour markets of some regions had disconcerting political, as well as social, implications. The result was the introduction after the late 1950s of many policy modifications aimed at strengthening the impact of intervention in regional economies. Indeed, the contrast between the 1950s and the 1960s was such that, for the purposes of policy evaluation, the two decades have often been equated with 'policy-off' and 'policy-on' periods. What is also noticeable is that the introduction of stronger policies was often accompanied by greater publicity for the view that improved efficiency in the use of national resources demanded the application of more effective regional measures. This owed something to advances in regional theory in the 1950s, but it was by no means unconnected with the fact that stronger policies were more expensive for the taxpayer to support and posed a greater threat to the growth potential of prosperous regions. These, and other political ramifications, have been considered at length by McHale and Shaber (1976).

THE EUROPEAN COMMUNITY AND REGIONAL POLICY

The contrast between the 1950s and the 1960s is also marked at the international level, for co-operation between countries to stimulate weak regional economies largely postdates the foundation of the European Economic Community. Despite this relatively late start, the Community's attack on regional problems has broadened rapidly, and financial assistance for area development is now channelled through three main agencies: the European Regional Development Fund (ERDF), the

European Investment Bank (EIB) and the European Coal and Steel Community (ECSC). All are well established but, as the following survey indicates, it is important to appreciate that progress towards community intervention did not take place according to an overall plan (Wallace, 1977; Talbot, 1978; Armstrong, 1979).

It was not intended that the ECSC, which was established by the Treaty of Paris in 1951, should become an agency permanently involved in regional economic planning. Apart from the political goal of achieving greater harmony in Western Europe in the early postwar period, its principal long-term role was taken to be the guidance of two vital industries towards higher production, greater efficiency and consistent profits. Yet what was envisaged from the outset was that in the 1950s redundancy problems could not be avoided as unprofitable facilities were closed and as capital was substituted for labour. These redundancies would be strongly concentrated in a relatively small number of regions, of which industrial southern Belgium was acknowledged to be the most severe example. Consequently, to cope with sharp adjustments in regional labour demand, the concept of transitional 'readaptation' assistance for workers was introduced. During the 1950s retraining schemes, the maintenance of displaced workers' earnings and subsidies for migration to areas of higher labour demand became major features of this readaptation policy, the financing of which was achieved by placing a levy on coal and steel industry turnover. Thus 'in these ways the ECSC was a social system intended to buffer the worker against the responsibility of bearing the cost of changes and win his acceptance of them' (Collins, 1975, p. 39).

By the late 1950s, however, it was apparent that early predictions concerning the future of the coal industry were extremely over-optimistic (Gordon, 1970). Petroleum products, the cost of which had decreased in real terms, had eaten into coal's markets; cheap coal imports were causing the indigenous industry to lose further ground; and by the end of 1959 it was known that a natural gas deposit important at the world scale lay under the northern Netherlands. Because the 1960s would undoubtedly be a decade of continuing far-reaching change, new regulations were introduced establishing worker readaptation as a permanent policy. But it was realised that this policy, as originally conceived, had its inadequacies. New industries were migrating to coalfield labour supplies at a disconcertingly slow rate; experience in France had shown that redundant workers were reluctant to migrate, even when some of the practical problems were smoothed by the ECSC; and the desirability of relocating labour was questioned because of the social dislocation and migration's effects on demand in the affected regions.

The response to these problems was that positive steps should be taken by the ECSC in the 1960s to accelerate the restructuring of coal- and steel-based economies by introducing new activities to them. Early in the decade, therefore, the ECSC's activities were extended to include the 'conversion' of problem areas, with financial restrictions dictating that aid should be offered in the form of loans rather than grants. Subsequently worker readaptation and area conversion have remained interrelated goals, but in the early 1960s conversion rapidly became the principal investment target. Between 1961 and 1967 the allocation of finance to conversion projects was more than twice that to the readaptation programme, and by 1980 the allocation ratio had risen to almost 4 : 1.

In contrast to the ECSC, the EIB was specifically created to deal with spatial development problems at the Community level. To some extent the motivation for this step was social, in as much as prosperity gaps within the Six were considered unjust, but the primary factor leading to the Bank's creation was the fear that regional problems would become a destabilising force undermining the Community's long-term political goals. It was predicted, for example, that an immediate effect of removing intra-Community tariff barriers would be increased competition for traditional industries in many relatively weak regions, competition they would be unable to resist. Similarly it was argued that steps towards monetary union might increase the disadvantages of many lagging regions because it would become impossible for national governments to increase their competitive edge in international markets by means of currency devaluations. When faced with these prospects, future governments might well be reluctant to implement Community policies, and in the light of this analysis the need was identified for an intervention agency able to counteract the danger that integration measures would accentuate spatial economic imbalance, cause political friction and block further progress towards the integration goal. This agency was to have wide-ranging power to assist all economic sectors and support public investment in infrastructure; although backed by the Community it was to have decision-making independence; and, while provision was made for its involvement in sectoral projects of benefit to more than one member country, the primary aim was to channel finance into the most needy regions. As with ECSC intervention, however, the climate of opinion was not in favour of large-scale sub-sidies in the form of grants, the cost of which would have fallen on governments already financially committed to their own regional strategies and to the Common Agricultural Pol-icy. Instead the way forward was seen to be the creation of a Community banking system which would borrow in the world's money markets and would then disburse its bor-rowings in the form of interest-bearing loans to selected pro-jects in priority regions. In this way capital flows were to be harnessed to promote interregional balance and political unity.

Articles 129 and 130 of the Treaty of Rome followed this philosophy closely in establishing the EIB, which has subse-quently been the subject of several reviews (Licari, 1970; EIB, 1978; Pinder, 1978). It is unnecessary to dwell on operational details at this point, but three general observations are appropriate. The first is that, because the repayment of finance raised in the money markets is guaranteed by member countries, the growth of the Bank's operations has proceeded with remarkably little difficulty. After an initial period of slow expansion between 1959 and 1965 the growth rate increased sharply, and even in the high-inflation years of the 1970s the real value of loans disbursed increased by 12 per cent a year. Secondly, although the Bank's activities have been diversified through, for example, the administration of loans to developing countries under the Lomé Convention, the focus on intra-Community development has remained the backbone of its activities: in 1981 internal allocations accounted for almost 90 per cent of all loans. And, thirdly, there has been close adherence to the principle of according priority to reg-ional development projects. These absorbed approximately 70 per cent of all lending in the Community in the early 1980s, and in the period 1958–78 the average was 75 per cent. Very rapidly, therefore, the EIB established itself as a major regional development agency and, to date, its experience in this field exceeds that of any other Community organisation.

Despite the swift expansion of the EIB's activities, the European Commission made it clear in the 1960s and early 1970s that its lack of influence on spatial development problems and programmes was unsatisfactory. Support for this view came from the European Parliament – for example, in the form of the Birchelbach and Bersani reports (European Parliament, 1963, 1966). But individual governments showed little enthusiasm for increasing the Commission's direct power, and the fact that the Commission failed to produce a detailed proposal for the pursuit of regional policy at the Community level did not further its cause.

In 1971 and 1972 the situation changed rapidly for political reasons. Discussion of monetary union widened the realisation of the regional implications of this particular Community policy (Williamson, 1975). It was increasingly argued that the Common Agricultural Policy benefited rich Community regions rather than poor ones (an accusation recently substantiated by the Commission's report *The Regions of Europe*; Commission of the European Communities, 1980a). And during negotiations for the first expansion of the Community the question of establishing a regional fund to be administered through the Commission became a major issue, chiefly as a result of pressure from Britain. At the Paris Summit of October 1972 a milestone was reached when member governments agreed to establish this fund by the end of 1973, a decision reinforced by the publication of the Commission's (1973) *Report on the Regional Problems of the Enlarged Community* (the Thomson Report). Yet the fund still faced turbulent political waters, most particularly in the form of the resurrection of German antipathy and a British Labour government's commitment to renegotiate entry to the Community. Between July 1973 and November 1974 no less than fourteen different funding arrangements were proposed by individual governments and the Commission, and deadlock was only avoided when Italy and Ireland threatened to withdraw from the December 1974 Summit if agreement was not immediately forthcoming. This precipitated the creation of the European

Regional Development Fund on an experimental three-year basis in March 1975 (Wallace, 1977). This was followed by its conversion into a permanent Community instrument from 1978 onwards on the basis of the Commission's (1977a) document 'Community regional policy: new guidelines'.

Since then the ERDF has been subject to regular annual funding under the main Community budget, and it has been restructured to accommodate Greece's accession in 1981. Until the early 1980s much of the pressure for further improvement continued to come from the European Parliament and the Commission, rather than from the Council of Ministers, while recurrent disagreements took place between the two sides over matters relating to the Fund's size and its control. In 1980, however, the Council of Ministers set in motion a new chain of events in an attempt to improve the effectiveness of this source of development aid. The outcome is likely to be a significant revision of the ERDF by the mid-1980s, and a detailed discussion of the Commission's proposals for the future of this aid agency has therefore been included in Chapter 5.

While the Community's intervention agencies remain separate, they share common ground in that they have all engaged in research into regional economic problems and their solution. Similarly, the desire to measure and improve policy effectiveness has motivated many investigations by planning agencies in member countries. Unfortunately the results of much of this research have been employed internally, without widespread circulation, but in recent years the flow of publications from the European Commission has been especially valuable in rectifying this shortcoming. Between 1973 and 1980, for example, the Commission issued no less than nineteen regional policy studies, a series drawing heavily on expertise both in Brussels and in Community members. None the less, the vast majority of the relevant literature has been published independently of official channels, although there is an important area of overlap in which researchers have been supported by official contracts and grants. More than any other groups, academic geographers and economists have been responsible for this independent and semi-independent work, and it is to the origins of their interest in the subject that we now turn.

The Rise of Regional Studies

In view of many geographers' current interest in regional problems, it is remarkable that in the early postwar period regional studies were extremely unfashionable. In many ways this attitude was a reaction to the prewar work of regional geographers, work which contributed to the growth of doubts about the utility of focusing primarily on the regional theme. The reasons for these doubts, which for many amounted to disenchantment, will become apparent if prewar approaches to regional geography, and especially the approaches pursued in Germany and France, are considered.

In France, where Vidal de la Blache exerted great influence over the discipline, the regional theme became increasingly central to the geographer's work in the early part of this century. In Germany the transition came slightly later, but when the change was made it was rapid, so that the interwar period was in general typified by intensive regional investigation. This surge of interest produced a large and varied literature (Hartshorne, 1939) from which two main tenets emerged. These were, first, the concept that regions exist as identifiable, finite entities and, secondly, the belief that geographers should take an all-embracing 'holistic' approach to the study of individual regions. Diligently pursued though they were, it is arguable that these preoccupations contributed more than any others to creating disenchantment with regional research.

A major pitfall inherent in the concept that regions exist as identifiable objects was a predisposition to interpret their operation in terms of closed, rather than open, systems. Even though the interwar years witnessed many examples of economic events in one part of the world leading to far-reaching consequences elsewhere, and even though this was a period in which the intranational and international movement of goods and people increased rapidly as a result of technological progress in land, sea and air transport, the role played by spatial interaction in the control of regional development processes was not given prominence. Meanwhile the barrier to progress raised by the holistic approach was its insistence that it is the geographer's task to deal with relationships between *all* phenomena in a study region, the argument being that these relationships make the region more than the sum of its parts. When the complexities of twentieth-century economies and societies are borne in mind it becomes apparent that this task was impossible, yet commitment to the holistic goal persisted and in many instances ensured that contributions to the regional literature were descriptive rather than explanatory. This encouraged the view that regional geography was an integrating activity that could do little more than draw together research undertaken in leading branches of the subject. Not unnaturally, therefore, these other branches increasingly appeared to offer the researcher more challenge and reward for his effort.

In an attempt to break more fertile ground R. E. Dickinson, an American geographer working largely in Europe, published *City, Region and Regionalism* in 1947. A basic theme of this work was that cities polarise economic and social life in a surrounding area, so that an understanding of any specific *city region* requires appreciation of complex interactions between the city and the area it animates. Viewing the region internally, therefore, the city-region philosophy relies on a dynamic functional interpretation, a stance which is extended to the question of external relationships. Thus city regions are not conceived as dominantly closed systems but as interacting forces, each of which affects, and is affected by, other regions in the system. Moreover, while regional boundaries may be drawn on a map for convenience they are not sacrosanct: they change with time and technological developments; contact between neighbouring regions implies the existence of transition zones; and recognition of the urban hierarchy leads towards the concept of overlapping 'nested' regions animated by cities occupying different ranks.

Despite its dynamic, innovative features, the city-region approach did not provide the main driving force behind the eventual resurgence of geographers' interest in regional studies. Broadly speaking this resurgence began in the early 1960s and grew rapidly into the 1970s, the trigger being the adoption of regional policies in many West European countries. This political movement provided a new focus for geographers: the study of regional development problems and the strategies employed to ameliorate them. Social relevance was a key attraction in this welfare approach (King and Clarke,

1978), and in the pursuit of this the constraints imposed by earlier regional work were rapidly discarded. This can be readily demonstrated with respect to the problem of regional definition. Despite some interest in employing mathematical techniques to establish regional boundaries, most geographers have preferred to work within the frameworks set by official planning regions or other administrative units employed by those engaged in regional planning. While it is true that this reflects pragmatism, in the sense that data availability is often geared to administrative frameworks, it also indicates an awareness of relationships between administrative and economic systems in late-twentieth-century society. Spatial administrative systems may not be ideal, but it is realistic to recognise that policies intended to influence economic development will be applied within them.

Because problem-orientated and policy-orientated approaches have made the work of geographers much more incisive, the study of regional development processes, 'surfaces' and policies can be regarded as a systematic branch of human geography with its own research frontier. But geography is not the only discipline to have experienced rapid change in this direction in the postwar period, for economics has given birth to a major sub-discipline concerned with regional economic systems. As might be anticipated, the goals of this emerging discipline were initially poorly defined, a characteristic stressed by both Meyer (1963) and Dubey (1964) in their surveys of the crystallisation of regional economics. Dubey, for example, suggests in his relatively brief paper that Myrdal, one of the major pioneers in this field, initially regarded the subject as the study of all regional problems from an economic viewpoint, while Meyer demonstrates that Myrdal was by no means alone in taking this very broad view. But other workers preferred to focus on narrower themes, and in particular, on the economic difficulties arising from the spatial immobility of unevenly distributed resources. Moreover, while economic considerations were naturally fundamental, the view that work in this field should be seen to have social relevance also became established. This was certainly the opinion of Meyer, whose attitudes directly influenced the definition of the new discipline advanced by Dubey in 1964. This definition (p. 28) embraced the understanding of regional economic problems and the concept of planned intervention on behalf of society:

> Regional economics is, therefore, the study, from the viewpoint of economics, of the differentiation and interrelationships of areas in a universe of unevenly distributed and imperfectly mobile resources, with particular emphasis on the planning of social overhead capital investments to mitigate the social problems created by these circumstances.

In practice government intervention has been much broader than this quotation's emphasis on social overhead capital would suggest, but a more important point is that Dubey's definition indicates the speed with which regional economics developed a concern for relevance and understanding. Richardson (1978a) has provided a recent overview of the subject, including an extensive bibliography, from which it is clear that subsequent progress has also been impressive. Admittedly, many of the advances have not been made in a specifically European context; as will become apparent in Chapter 2, the movement grew rapidly on both sides of the Atlantic, and considerable attention was given to the imbalance between Third World and advanced economies. Yet many of the concepts and theories relating to regional functioning and regional interrelationships have been applied subsequently in Western Europe and, although there are dangers in transposing ideas derived in one part of the world to areas with very different economic, social and political backgrounds, there is no doubt that on balance the adoption of these ideas has done much to improve insights into the nature of European regional problems.

Although a distinction can be drawn between the revival of geographical interest in regional research and the foundation of regional economics, in some respects this division has become artificial. Geographers have adopted (and adapted) regional economic theories and techniques in order to improve their understanding of how regional systems function, interact and malfunction. Conversely, some regional economists have become less disposed to set their work in an entirely theoretical context, preferring instead to evaluate and modify concepts in the light of real-world experience. Economists and geog-

raphers have swelled the ranks of the regional economic planning profession, while the move in favour of interdisciplinary
work has been typified by the journal *Regional Studies*, a
forum established to promote discussion between professions.
This cross-fertilisation has undoubtedly been fruitful in
academic circles and, although Wullkopf and Pearce (1977)
have argued that researchers must continue to adapt in order
to contribute more effectively to policy development, the work
of at least some academics has influenced policy design and
application. This is particularly true with respect to economists; as Claval (1975) has emphasised, in Europe the names of
Boudeville, Klaassen, Paelinck and Davin are well known in
this connection.

The remainder of this book provides a commentary on the
outcome of academic and political approaches to the problems
of spatial inequality. Chapters 2 and 3 review regional
development theories and their contribution to our understanding of the causes and nature of spatial variations in prosperity. Here the initial focus is on interregional theory and its
implications for Community expansion, after which attention
turns to intraregional theory and the role of private and public
sectors in the development process. Against this theoretical
background Chapter 4 charts the rise of regional policies, considers the methods employed in the attempt to correct major
imperfections in the development surface and compares
national strategies with those of the Community. Chaper 5
explores the question of policy assessment, the difficulties
inherent in the assessment process and the prospects for
further progress in an expanding Community experiencing
severe recession. Finally, the bibliography offers an introduction to further reading on this major subject.

2 Regional Imbalance and Community Expansion

Interregional Relationships – Economic Convergence or Divergence?

Interregional theories attempt to account for, and to predict the future of, broad interregional development contrasts observable within and between countries. Theoretical arguments relating to interregional growth processes have been dominated by two schools of thought. On the one hand it has been claimed that long-term development trends lead to a state of regional equilibrium. According to this thesis the natural operation of economic mechanisms achieves balanced functioning within individual regional economies and also gives rise to the elimination of major interregional development contrasts. Conversely the disequilibrium school maintains that theoretical reasoning and available evidence point to the conclusion that long-term trends frequently widen existing development gaps. While some regions prosper, others suffer the handicaps of under-utilised resources, depressed incomes and restricted employment opportunities; underachievement is the lot of such areas, an outcome that is in neither the regional nor the national interest.

Emphasis will not be given here to the standard equilibrium argument for, as Holland (1976a) has stressed, those who have advocated equilibrium models have often argued in very abstract terms, adopting assumptions departing seriously from real-world conditions. Since the mid-1950s, however, one version of the equilibrium view has been argued which not only encompasses important characteristics of the real world but also rejects the dogma that the unfettered operation of market forces necessarily leads to regional equality. It is with consideration of this argument that the examination of interregional theory will begin.

The version of equilibrium theory in question is directly attributable to the economist Hirschman, and in particular to his book *The Strategy of Economic Development* (1958). Hirschman's outlook is far from that adopted by the traditional equilibrium school, rooted as it is in the recognition of contrasting regional resource endowments and development levels. A fundamental aspect of his theory is that 'the emergence of growing points and therefore of differences in development between regions is inevitable' (p. 187), and much of the ingenuity in his ideas lies in the incorporation of this principle into an equilibrium approach. Couching his argument in terms of North versus South, Hirschman reasons that disequilibrium is an essential stage in the journey towards equilibrium. Regions advantageously located or endowed (the North) must develop first and, moreover, must do so partly at the expense of less-favoured areas (the South). The process of Southern impoverishment Hirschman calls polarisation, a term implying the movement of resources from South to North, and it is assumed that these resources are likely to cover a wide range – physical, financial and human. For example, raw materials may be exported to the North for processing, with a consequent loss of manufacturing employment and value added in the South; profits accumulated by Southern economic activity may also be part of the polarised flow, attracted to the North by a multiplicity of high-yielding investment opportunities; and it is envisaged also that young workers, the well educated and those with entrepreneurial abilities will be drawn from the South in disproportionate numbers, so weakening still further its ability for self-help.

Hirschman also hypothesises, however, that expansion in the North gradually enables the advanced region to reverse Southern trends by means of external stimulation. To some extent this process can be expected to work through the labour market: although well-qualified people are lost in disproportionate numbers, the majority of migrants are ordinary workers leaving the South. Their departure increases Southern labour productivity and earnings, so giving rise to higher disposable incomes and improved per capita demand. But the most significant stimulation effects (termed 'trickling down' by

Hirschman) are likely to be, first, the North's increasing tendency to satisfy demand by purchases in the South and, secondly, the advanced region's investments in the South. To some extent, it is argued, the emergence of this investment flow will be caused by attempts to expand the output of products required by the North. But in addition it is assumed that it will be generated by the realisation that diseconomies, such as high labour, land and building costs, can be associated with locations in hyperactive, congested regions. Whatever the precise nature of the trickling down, however, it is hypothesised that it will significantly improve Southern income, a development which in turn should stimulate other forms of employment, thereby firmly establishing the movement towards equilibrium.

Optimistic though it may seem, Hirschman's theory imposes an important condition to be fulfilled before trickling down can predominate over polarisation. This condition is that complementarity between regional economies is essential if an advanced region is to transmit effective growth impulses to less-advanced areas. In other words, trickling down would 'gain the upper hand if the North had to rely to an important degree on Southern products for its expansion' (p. 189). This is clearly a crucial qualification, for in many real-world situations the resource base of a lagging region might simply be unsuitable for the production of goods required by the North. Alternatively, even if appropriate resources were present or could be obtained, a Southern economy might be too inelastic to respond sufficiently rapidly to the North's demands. In either event the advanced region would be likely to turn elsewhere for its requirements, an option facilitated by modern transportation, in which case trickling down would be unable to compensate for polarisation forces. Weak stimulation might continue to occur in the form of, for example, higher productivity arising from the North's attraction of surplus labour, but Hirschman's view is that 'the stage would be set for a prolonged split of the country into a progressive and a depressed area' (p. 189). Moreover, continued advance in the North might well intensify polarisation effects as a result of increasing economies of scale in manufacturing. As these became progressively more important, the fact that low unit costs were obtainable outside the South would reduce still further the attractions of investing in the region. Northern economies of scale would also enable that area to undermine the viability of producers already operating in the lagging region. In this case the North would eat into Southern markets, effectively increasing the polarisation of demand on the Northern economy.

From this discussion it is apparent that Hirschman's analysis is by no means one-sided. Given interregional complementarity he inclines to the equilibrium view; without it he is pessimistic, believing disequilibrium to be the likely outcome. This flexibility, which is often overlooked in favour of stressing his equilibrium views, is an attractive feature of his ideas; neither development path is inevitable, but a regional system will tend to follow one or other of the courses according to the circumstances prevailing at a particular time.

Williamson (1965) has argued that equilibrium tendencies can be observed in the regional systems of several European countries if the analysis is based on the relative variation of regional per capita incomes around the national average. Judged by this criterion, the Netherlands and West Germany showed clear signs of convergence in the early postwar period, while in France and Italy the indications were that stability, rather than divergence, was the prevailing force. This evidence apparently strengthens the case for accepting the equilibrium view, but Williamson's findings must be qualified. For example, postwar convergence in regional per capita incomes may have reflected to a considerable degree the rise of the welfare state, with its capacity for generating interregional income transfers (Commission of the European Communities, 1980a). Connected with this is the point that per capita *income* is by no means synonymous with per capita *output*, a criterion which may have behaved differently over the same period. And, as Williamson himself stressed, 'It is quite possible and hardly uncommon that a period of convergence in regional income *per capita relative to a national average* may at the same time be one of increasing absolute differentials'. Indeed, his paper provides evidence of this phenomenon with respect to Italy and, most especially, Sweden.

Given these caveats, it becomes easier to understand why most space economists have felt constrained to agree with

Hirschman's pessimistic divergence scenario. In doing so they have bolstered the argument advanced by Myrdal's frequently cited book *Economic Theory and Underdeveloped Regions* (1957) which, like Hirschman's work, presents the case for regarding interregional relationships in terms of opposing spatial forces. Myrdal's terminology is different – polarisation and trickling down are called 'backwash' and 'spread' effects – but his main departure from Hirschman's theory is in his emphasis on the improbability of advanced regions effectively stimulating lagging areas. Similarly Friedmann (1966, 1972) stresses that historical evidence does not support the equilibrium model and argues strongly that polarising forces are likely to be dominant. Building on these foundations the disequilibrium school has grown considerably, and there is no doubt that since the mid-1960s it has been far more widely supported than has the equilibrium approach. Moreover, the consequences of this have not been confined to academic circles. Hirschman, Myrdal and Friedmann have all related their theoretical work to the question of government strategies intended to control polarisation and encourage trickling down and, even though the weight of their interventionist arguments has been directed at less developed countries, the fundamental message has not fallen upon deaf ears elsewhere. The basic principles and conclusions have been transposed to advanced areas, and to Western Europe in particular, where they have been used by many administrations to provide academic justification for regional policies.

INTERREGIONAL DISEQUILIBRIUM AND BEHAVIOURAL THEORY

The discussion of disequilibrium theory has assumed that contrasts in regional prosperity emerge entirely as a result of economic processes and rational decisions taken by individuals. According to these assumptions physical, financial and human resources flow to regions experiencing strong growth because businessmen, investors and perhaps even potential migrant workers carefully evaluate opportunities in competing regions and act on their conclusions. It is, however, highly unlikely that interregional factor allocation is purely the outcome of this type of rigorous decision-making process, the basis of which would be the detailed and accurate assessment of all market forces. The latter are certainly significant, but it is arguable that a deeper understanding of regional problems can be gained if attention is given to the ability of individuals to perceive geographical space objectively and to gather and evaluate information efficiently. Although these behavioural questions have not been fully explored with respect to the perception of regional economic opportunities, the case for a behavioural view of regional problems can be readily demonstrated.

Even though the need to study perception and behaviour only became widely accepted in the 1970s, Hirschman stressed the importance of these factors in the mid-1950s. His discussion is brief, but he identifies three fundamental and interrelated influences on regional development. First, the extent to which entrepreneurs evaluate in detail the economic advantages of growth regions is questioned. It is clear that Hirschman believes that locations in such regions are often chosen or maintained primarily because the regions in question are seen to be successful, the assumption being that success is in some way contagious. Secondly, he suggests that detailed analysis of locations in advanced regions would certainly show them to be advantageous, but not as strongly advantageous as businessmen believe. Thirdly, he argues that over-estimation of the benefits of locations in growth regions lead to distorted views of the investment opportunities that in reality are available elsewhere. In this way lagging regions become seriously undervalued, and entrepreneurs with 'a special kind of boldness' are required to overcome this hurdle (p. 184).

The essence of Hirschman's argument, which is largely endorsed by Myrdal and Friedmann, is that businessmen and investors possess 'mental maps' of spatial opportunity that deviate markedly from reality. In behavioural terms, information transmitted by the objective (i.e. real) environment is filtered by the minds of individuals, with the degree of filtration varying from person to person, so that everyone creates his or her behavioural or 'task' environment. Repeated exposure to particular features of the objective environment will, however, increase the probability of their inclusion in the behavioural environment and, since people are most frequently exposed to those parts of the objective environment that are in the immediate vicinity, distortions of mental maps away from reality are bound to occur. But mental maps are not only the outcome of first-hand experience. They are also influenced by information gained, for example, through the media, and it is likely that this type of information-gathering is important in encouraging polarisation. Consistent exposure to the general idea that conditions are more attractive in another region is likely to add that region to the mental maps of businessmen and potential migrant workers, so counterbalancing the pull of the familiar home region. Similarly, the glowing opinions of relatives, friends, or business associates in other regions may be sufficient to modify the map.

Empirical evidence of the importance of distorted mental maps has been provided by Downs and Stea (1977) and Gould and White (1974). Working largely with school-leavers and students, Gould and White have given particular attention to the cognition of national space in the United States and Britain. From their investigations it is clear that in the large majority of cases individuals give prominence to the areas with which they are familiar, while the level of awareness falls rapidly outside these relatively limited zones. Important additional perspectives on perception, behaviour and industrial location have been provided by Pred (1967) and Gold (1980). This work has stressed that, as well as being influenced by the filtering of information from the objective environment, business decisions are heavily dependent on the ability of decision-makers to analyse the incomplete information fields that are available to them. Time constraints, character, educational background, age, experience and many other factors are all likely to be influential in this respect. However, the fact that these influences may be important does not mean that decision-makers are completely irrational or entirely subjective in their approaches. More probably they are at least partially aware of personal shortcomings and gaps in their knowledge, with the result that the attempt is made to work towards generally rational goals against a background of uncertainty. Uncertainty breeds caution and this, again, can have spatial consequences. Demonstrably successful regional economies are likely to benefit from investment to a disproportionate degree because of their apparent safety, while hesitancy over conditions likely to be encountered in lagging regions will damp down the 'special kind of boldness' identified by Hirschman as being necessary to appreciate the opportunities they offer.

Once it is accepted that behavioural as well as economic factors play a part in interregional disequilibrium processes, an important conclusion follows: strategies designed to improve interregional balance will be incomplete if they focus on economic considerations alone. Attention must also be given to overcoming the psychological barriers to development in lagging areas and, as Chapter 4 demonstrates, the realisation of this has had important consequences for regional promotion policies.

Centres, Peripheries, Growth Poles and Regional Differentiation

Returning to analyses of regional problems that are couched in North–South terms, it is necessary to consider pitfalls inherent in the application of this approach in a European context. Much of Friedmann's (1966) discussion of North–South relationships is presented in centre–periphery terms, the centre being equivalent to the advanced North while the periphery represents the disadvantaged, lagging South. In the years since Friedmann discussed interregional development problems in this fashion the centre–periphery, or core–periphery model has achieved considerable popularity, having been applied in many parts of the world on widely differing scales. In Western Europe the adoption of this model has been widespread. At the national level the peripherality of the Mezzogiorno in the Italian 'national space' has frequently been noted as a factor contributing to spatial economic imbalance, as has that of Scotland and Northern Ireland in the UK as a whole. Similarly in France the notion of 'Paris et le désert français' has been highly influential in moulding academic and political attitudes to French regional problems while, despite their small size, both Belgium and the Netherlands include regions considered to be disadvantaged by remoteness from the present-day heart of their respective national economies. Moreover, with increasing acceptance that the EEC is a genuine, if far from perfect, organisation whose tasks include safeguarding the welfare of the Community as a whole, there has been an understandable tendency to add an international perspective to the discussion of peripherality phenomena. Seers, Schaffer and Kiljunen (1979) have provided a particularly useful investigation of this theme with their book *Underdeveloped Europe*. Similarly, Keeble, Owens and Thompson (1981) have demonstrated statistical relationships between many adverse economic criteria and remoteness from the Community's economic core. As McCrone (1975) has argued, however, although the scale flexibility of the centre–periphery model may be attractive, there is the danger that placing too much reliance upon this concept will lead to grossly oversimplified views of both the geography and the structural characteristics of European regional problems.

With respect to geographical oversimplification, the prime pitfall likely to be encountered is that of viewing the EEC as an economic heartland (for example, Paris–London–Randstad–Ruhr–Frankfurt) set in a relatively homogeneous periphery. While there is obviously a measure of truth in such an interpretation, it is essential to recognise diversity in both the periphery and the core. Application of the centre–periphery model at both the national and regional levels goes some way towards achieving this, particularly by emphasising that peripherality can usefully be regarded as a 'nested concept' in which peripheries lie within each other in the manner of Russian dolls. However, although this improvement emphasises that there are many variations on the peripherality theme, it does not fully underline the range of economic problems to be found outside national and international core zones. Likewise it leaves largely intact the implication that the centre, the economic heartland, is an essentially uniform region of high prosperity. The core of Western Europe is in fact a mosaic of regions which have developed by following a variety of paths and which display significant differences in economic health. These differences are to a great extent the product of interaction between historical legacy and late-twentieth-century global economic conditions, and it would be a mistake to underrate them. To suggest in the Nord coalfield, in industrial southern Belgium, or in the Dutch province of Limburg that local prosperity and employment opportunities are equal to those in nearby capital regions would be to invite a sharp reaction.

Oversimplified views of the structural economic problems typifying areas outside core regions are likely to arise from a failure to appreciate the implications of those aspects of economic theory encompassed by the growth-pole model. Growth-pole theory was developed by the French economic theorist François Perroux (1950, 1955), the essence of his argument being that from time to time activities capable of achieving far-reaching economic growth emerge and rapidly become significant influences in the development process. These influences operate in a variety of ways. For example, an emergent leading industry is likely to become a significant employer in its own right, absorbing labour reserves, attracting labour from less productive activities and significantly increasing the purchasing power of a population. Increased purchasing power is likely to stimulate consumer-orientated industries, but in all probability the leading industry will exert stimulating effects quite separate from those to be expected from the normal consumer-demand chain. Some of these effects should appear on the input side of the equation, for the leading industry is unlikely to be self-contained with respect to all its requirements. In this way growth may be induced in existing supply industries and, equally important, the nature of the required inputs may be such that new industries must be called into being to fulfil the leader's demands. On the output side of the equation a new leading activity's products, which will be based on the latest technology available, are likely to have implications for pre-existing industries. Some may be superseded but it is probable that others will be revolutionised and set on the road to far-reaching expansion. Moreover, largely as a consequence of the application of new technology, the leading industry's outputs may well become the inputs for industries manufacturing entirely new products. These, too, will contribute to growth, but they will also bring about modernisation in the prevailing economic structure. In time, therefore, an economy affected by this process will not only be propelled by the growth pole (that is, the leading activity and its associated industries) to higher output levels; it will also evolve a modernised structure and product range that will offer significant advantages over competing economies.

Much of Perroux's theory is related to non-spatial economics rather than their geographical outcome, but the last quarter of his influential 1955 paper touches upon the spatial consequences of growth-pole development, with far-reaching implications for the classification of problem regions today. As with the remainder of the paper, the argument is not illustrated by specific examples, but the fact that Perroux was primarily concerned with long-term economic evolution suggests that it is necessary to interpret his ideas in an historico-spatial context. In particular it is useful to consider Europe's leading industries in the second half of the nineteenth century, such as coal, iron and steel, engineering, carbo-chemicals and textiles; and, because of Perroux's emphasis on inter-industry relationships, we must think also of the numerous linkages with 'downstream' consumers of semi-manufactured products and with 'upstream' activities whose products and services allowed the main propulsive industries to survive and expand. Although there were obvious variations from country to country, these complex industrial groupings were fundamentally responsible for the dramatic nineteenth-century progress of the Western European economies (Milward and Saul, 1977). But, despite their powerful nature, the major growth-pole industries were not without important limitations, particularly with respect to the question of location. Especially in their all-important formative years, these activities were largely unable to employ disjointed and low-capacity transportation systems as a lever to overcome the polarising pull of physical and human resources. Consequently industries that were grouped, to use Perroux's term, in 'economic space' were obliged to concentrate in geographical space as well. As the century neared its end improved transportation, especially in the form of comprehensive national and international railway systems, weakened technical locational constraints. But the constraints were by no means eliminated, and by this time the concentration of capital in major industrial areas, and manufacturers' perceptions of what constituted appropriate industrial locations, were powerful forces working to smother major locational changes. So were strategic factors, which continued to encourage vital industries to focus on sources of war materials. Early industrial centres therefore became the foundations of the great coal-, engineering-, and textile-based industrial conurbations which, had the centre–periphery model existed at the turn of the century, would have been regarded as economic heartlands polarising national and, especially in the case of colonial powers, international resources.

At the other extreme, substantial parts of Western Europe did not experience this take-off, either because their physical and human resources were inadequate, or because their locations failed to fit them for the role of industrial regions. In these areas agriculture continued to provide an unusually high proportion of regional employment, although succeeding decades have witnessed a steady change that has given many present-day regions an employment structure chiefly composed of service activities and low-order industry. This evolutionary process has typically given rise to a type of region that may be termed the low-intensity economy. Frequently it is too weak to prevent endemic polarisation towards stronger regions, but in absolute terms this problem is not usually spectacular compared with the recent fortunes of the major nineteenth-century industrial regions, which are now far past their prime. In these areas products have been superseded, technologies have become outdated and employment has contracted sharply. As Massey (1979) has emphasised, this process has sometimes proceeded so far that traditional regional economic structures have been modified almost beyond recognition. Although modernisation has by no means bypassed these economies completely, the pace of adjustment has been sufficiently slow for them to become industrial problem regions; and the control of new industrialisation has often been based elsewhere, so that old industrial districts tended to assume a colonial relationship with more thrusting leader regions.

Given this background of highly dynamic temporal-spatial interaction it is clear that, at least in the European context, the label 'peripheral' has the capacity to disguise fundamental differences between regions that were once centres, but are no longer, and those that have never enjoyed that status. The former struggle against the consequences of handsome nineteenth-century endowment with Perroux's growth-pole industries: strong population concentrations, outmoded and declining traditional industries, pollution in a number of guises and widespread physical decay, especially of inner-urban areas. In contrast, regions that have never experienced

large-scale take-off have missed the benefits of major industrialisation, but have also avoided the disadvantages following
in its wake. Although southern Italy is an important exception
to the general rule, the economic problems generally revolve
around low populations and the need for widespread growth
on a modest scale, whereas the industrial problem regions
require concentrated large-scale growth to offset far-reaching
decline. The two sets of circumstances are generically quite
different, and it is therefore essential for our understanding of
regional systems that we should modify the simple twofold
classification arising from the centre–periphery model. At the
very least a threefold classification is required, one which
retains the concept of leader regions but clearly distinguishes
the origins and problems of low-intensity economies and
industrial problem regions.

Although this threefold classification is based on economic
structure and dynamism, the question of regional classification can be approached from a variety of other viewpoints.
This subject has been examined by Guttenberg (1977) and a
full survey is unnecessary here. However, three further observations are appropriate with respect to the relationship between regional classification and development issues. The first
is that economic problems are in some instances responses to
political factors, especially in the case of frontier regions (Burtenshaw, 1976a). These can lay claim to be placed in a special
problem category, partly as a consequence of their peripherality to their respective national territories, partly because international boundaries can be disruptive influences on co-
ordinated development in the divided areas, and partly
because development levels are sometimes substantially different on either side of a border. Since the Community came
into existence the problems of frontier regions have received
considerable attention: many loans for development projects
have been forthcoming from the European Investment Bank,
and there are a number of pilot projects to improve co-
ordinated development, such as that for the Eems–Dollart
region straddling part of the West German-Netherlands border.
As Husain (1981) has emphasised, however, problems arising
from frontier locations are not confined to borders separating
Community members. The Iron Curtain disrupted economic
interrelationships along its entire length, the consequences

being particularly evident with respect to the port of Hamburg, which lost a high proportion of its 'natural' hinterland. Compensation for this disruption has been costly and difficult, and progress has been heavily dependent on policy measures adopted by local and national governments.

Secondly, it is useful to recognise that some regions, which are often overlooked because they have not generated major physical or economic development handicaps, possess economies that are distinct from those that give rise to well-recognised regional problems. Like the problem regions, these 'normal' regions are integral components of their respective regional systems and they contribute to a key feature of those systems: competition for growth and investment resources. Within individual countries, and within the Community as a whole, all types of region are in constant competition for available growth, and against this background the process of regional classification can be seen as a step towards elucidating the spatial cut and thrust of economic life.

Thirdly, however, we must remind ourselves that this rationalisation is in many ways an artificial device applied to facilitate our understanding of highly complex interrelationships. While it may be helpful to conceptualise competition as a struggle between major types of region, in open regional systems all regions compete with each other as best they can and, indeed, competition for growth is a normal occurrence within, as well as between, regions.

Interregional Processes and Community Expansion

Community expansion by the accession of Greece, Spain and Portugal in the 1980s is a highly topical issue that has naturally generated a substantial literature (Commission of the European Communities, 1979a; Deubner, 1980; Ferreira, 1978; Shlaim and Yannopoulos, 1976; Wallace and Edwards, 1976; Yannopoulos, 1977). It is not the intention here to provide a comprehensive review of the political, economic and social pros and cons of expansion, but it is appropriate to consider, in the light of the earlier theoretical discussion, the implications of accession for the Community's regional system. Above all, these suggest that centre–periphery relationships should be given much more attention in the immediate future.

This conclusion may be reached by considering the place of manufacturing in the regional systems of Greece, Spain and Portugal. Especially in Spain and Portugal postwar policies deliberately cushioned existing industry and encouraged new activities, often financed by foreign investment, that were disposed to use the host countries as producing rather than marketing areas. As a result, although in Greece manufacturing accounts for little more than a third of GDP, in Spain the equivalent figure is approximately 42 per cent, and the Portuguese figure (45 per cent) is in fact slightly higher than the average for the Nine. Relatively effective though industrialisation policies were in macroeconomic terms, however, they largely ignored the issue of the regional distribution of growth; only in Spain has any substantial attention been given to additional policies to achieve balanced regional development, and even the Spanish efforts have not progressed far (Lasuén, 1974; Richardson, 1975). Consequently, development patterns displaying many of the characteristics of the centre–periphery model have become firmly established.

Much of the new industrialisation has gravitated to relatively compact regions corresponding with the 'centre' concept, leaving wide peripheries displaying the chief structural features of low-intensity economies: modest development of traditional industries, often related to the agricultural sector, and an unusually high dependence on agriculture itself. Polarisation, particularly of population resources, typifies these centre–periphery systems. Population loss is now common in central and western parts of Spain, in Portugal the eastern and central regions are being drained in this way, and the impact is particularly pronounced in regions unfortunate enough to occupy the Spanish-Portuguese border. Similarly, marked population decline has been a recent feature of five out of seven Greek statistical regions. This partly reflects the loss of people drawn into the international migrant-worker system, a point also relevant to Iberian population developments, but the principal migrant stream has focused on the Athens–Piraeus leader region.

Increased emphasis on the problem of centre–periphery relationships may also be anticipated as a result of agriculture's labour-intensive nature in Mediterranean countries. (In 1979 this sector employed only 7·6 per cent of the working population of the Nine, 19·5 per cent in Spain, 30·6 per cent in Portugal and 30·8 per cent in Greece.) Without intensive investment designed to overcome climatic limitations, to restructure output away from surplus commodities and to modernise holdings, it is unrealistic to envisage a significant reduction in rural–urban income disparities in the new members. Moreover, even allowing for much of this investment to come from Community as well as national funds, the financial and technical resources required to achieve widespread progress could only be made available over many decades. Also significant is the probability that where agricultural modernisation is undertaken it will achieve reductions in labour intensity. Rural restructuring is often associated with agricultural employment decline, a phenomenon contributing both to local demand for alternative employment and to population polarisation towards regions perceived to have higher labour requirements.

Although interregional disequilibrium in the centre–periphery mould presents an immediate challenge to politicians and economic planners in Greece, Spain and Portugal, its implications for the future of the Community may be even more far-reaching. A small number of modest leader regions will have been grafted on to the Community's regional system by the late 1980s, but the major part of the expansion will have been achieved by the addition of low-intensity industrial and agricultural economies. This implies the emergence of an increasingly sharp North/South dichotomy between northern and southern parts of the Community, a division which may be demonstrated by reference to output-per-head data. Before expansion the ratio between output per head in the richest and poorest Community regions was 6:1. After expansion this ratio will have risen to 12:1, and there will be many regions with ratios worse than the previous 6:1 figure. In addition the regional economies of the new members will be exposed to the impact of the Common Market (Marquand, 1980a), and it is therefore clear that major problems will confront those concerned with the formulation and implementation of national and Community regional policy. The current recession raises the question of whether the financial resources and economic impetus necessary to ameliorate these problems will be forthcoming. If they are not, the tendency may be for the new members to join with southern Italy to form a politically disaffected bloc accounting for 46 per cent of the Community's area, 36 per cent of its population and only 20 per cent of its GDP.

Economic circumstances within such a bloc would naturally vary from country to country, and it would therefore be unwise to conclude that its members would necessarily occupy identical standpoints and present a consistently united front when attempting to influence long-term Community strategy. In the field of international trade, for example, a distinction may readily be drawn between Italy and the new members. Throughout the Community's existence Italy has never experienced a major trade deficit with the remainder of the EEC whereas Greece, Spain and Portugal have all had significant negative trade balances with the Nine, at least with respect to visible earnings. Even though the Mediterranean countries cannot be regarded as a completely united group, however, the GDP figures quoted above enhance the impression of core versus periphery. The European Commission's attitude to this is encapsulated in its emphasis on 'the Mediterranean Challenge', and there is no doubt that the fundamental issues are clear. Will southern Community members make increasingly strident demands for regional policy to deal with the problem of North/South disequilibrium? And, if so, will this prove to be a source of confrontation and tension threatening the stability of the Community itself?

3 Internal Processes and External Relationships

It was suggested in Chapter 2 that, useful though the centre–periphery model may be as an aid to the rationalisation of interregional relationships, it can be misleading to apply the concept uncritically in the complex European context. The particular problems identified was the model's tendency to overlook contrasts of economic structure which have given rise to problem regions, but this is by no means the sole objection that can be raised. For example, by emphasising interregional relationships the model does not stress the complexity of internal economic processes, their relationships with a region's capacity to generate 'export' earnings and the diverse nature of the export sector. Similarly, the significance of financial flows from all types of region is under-estimated, while a preoccupation with the private sector leads to serious undervaluation of the role of public expenditure, even though this is now a major component of regional economic systems in all advanced countries. This list is not exhaustive, but the items on it are central issues, and this chapter therefore aims to work towards a more elaborate view of Europe's regional economies by consideration of these themes.

Internal Processes and Regional Export Earnings

Cumulative causation theory, which may be traced back to Myrdal (1957) and which may be used to elucidate both intraregional and interregional processes, assumes that certain firms or industries play a leading role in a regional economy because of their propensity to establish backward and forward linkages with other firms and industries. It is also assumed that the dependent, as well as the leading, activities will have requirements which lead to an elaboration of the linkage system and that, as long as the products of the linkage chains are readily assimilated by markets inside or outside the region, conditions will be appropriate for growth. The latter, it is suggested, can take a variety of forms, such as the expansion of existing activities, the attraction and creation of new firms, and population expansion caused by the attraction of workers to share in the region's prosperity. With growth established, the argument continues, additional labour resources and the development of good supportive services may in turn prove attractive to other industries and, because of general success and prosperity, investment finance for further regional expansion should be readily available. In this way it is hypothesised that successful regions are able to generate productive capacity and other resources, and it is this process of growth generation throughout an extended time period that lies at the centre of the concept of cumulative causation.

It will be apparent from this brief outline and from the discussion in Chapter 2 that this concept has much in common with growth-pole theory. Because growth-pole industries are, by definition, major expanding activities with a considerable propensity to generate forward and backward linkages, they clearly have potential as agents in the process of cumulative causation. Detailed studies of this potential are not numerous, but one recent investigation of considerable interest has examined the car industry and its component suppliers in Britain's West Midlands (Crompton, Barlow and Downing, 1976). This study found that in the mid-1970s more than 800 component suppliers within the region were linked with the car manufacturers, the estimated total employment of these suppliers being approximately 265,000. As is often the case with linked activities, however, most of the suppliers were not entirely dependent on the car industry for their market; indeed, many of the firms were actively pursuing market-diversification policies. After allowing for this, 103,000 workers in the component industry were considered to be directly dependent on car production, compared with 100,000 working in the car-assembly plants themselves. Influential though growth-pole industries may have been in the regional growth process, however, it is important to remember that they often display highly uneven location patterns, so that their main effects are normally felt in a limited number of regions. Consequently, although all regions experience cumulative causation in some degree, those with the greatest endowment of growth-pole activities can be expected to produce the most effective cumulative performance. While economic planners in European development areas have pursued the broad goal of employment creation, therefore, it is hardly surprising that opportunities to attract firms in industries believed to conform with the growth-pole concept have been viewed with special favour.

In addition to the multiplication of growth by the repercussive generation of linked businesses, the cumulative causation model hypothesises the existence of a further set of relationships within a regional economy, the basis of which is the demand created by the regional labour force and its dependants. Here the essential principle, again touched upon in Chapter 2, is that expenditure by the population' will multiply the employment opportunities available by cultivating activities oriented to satisfying regional 'residentiary' demand. Large-scale employment on the part of leading industries, for example, will generate demand in the form of wages and salaries pumped regularly into the economy, week by week, month by month. Residentiary activities, it is argued, will exist to satisfy this demand, and the size of these demand-oriented activities will be related, among other things, to the size and number of the leading industries. Wages and salaries paid by residentiary activities will also contribute to demand, however, so that the residentiary sector will be stimulated still further and, since this stimulation will result in further wage and salary payments, a repeating cycle will be established.

Although this basic multiplier mechanism is closely related to demand-oriented industry, the concept is also very relevant to the non-manufacturing sector of a regional economy. A proportion of demand arising from wage and salary flows will be for the services of people with particular skills or training, such as those in the medical, teaching, banking and legal professions. Service employment, especially in the form of wholesaling and retailing, must also exist to facilitate the transfer of products from manufacturer to consumer; and, since it is unrealistic to envisage regions as closed systems, the service activities will be intimately concerned with the import, distribution and sale of commodities that a region's residentiary industries are unable to supply. Thus the assumption is that the multiplier effect, working within the cumulative causation process, is capable of expanding and broadening regional economies by generating higher levels of activity in secondary and tertiary businesses. Conversely it is possible to envisage the possibility of the multiplier effect weakening as major propulsive industries progress into decline, a theme examined by Brownrigg (1980). Whether this trend is likely to become significant depends to some extent on a region's ability to generate or attract replacement productive activities; but a further factor that must be considered is the degree of modification that has been brought about in regional economic systems by the rise of the welfare state. We shall return to the issue of the state's supportive role in the closing section of this chapter.

It is apparent that the working of the multiplier can be seen as a process achieving the recycling of purchasing power in the form of demand. Beyond this, however, it has been argued that the impact of the multiplier varies with the volume of finance available to fuel demand, a conclusion that has led to the assertion that a region's prosperity is, at least in part, a reflection of its ability to generate external earnings. It is to this assumption, encapsulated in export-base theory, that we now turn.

The export-base concept, also known as staple theory, proposes that successful regional economies feed on other economies by exporting products to them in large quantities and receiving in return financial flows that activate intraregional demand in a variety of ways. The development of this basic argument has been particularly associated with studies of the economic history of North America, where it has been claimed that the colonisation and subsequent economic take-off of a number of regions were closely related to the exploitation of resources under the stimulus of demand from external markets (Stabler, 1968). Taking a broad view of the European scene it is possible to point to similar experience. Leading nineteenth-century industries such as coal, steel, engineering and textiles concentrated in relatively restricted regions from which they served major external markets. This process has been studied in detail by Gillet (1969) in the context of the Nord and Pas-de-Calais coalfields of France, and Warren (1976) has underlined the fact that, as early as the turn of the century, it was not uncommon for localities to be acutely aware of the extent to which their income was dependent on the behaviour of customers outside the region. Despite some historical underpinning, however, export-base theory has been the subject of considerable criticism, summarised by Richardson (1978b). From this it is clear that, if it is to be useful as a key to understanding modern regional economies, the character of the export sector must be elaborated and clarified.

One way in which it is constructive to broaden the export-base concept is to recognise that activities which do not physically produce goods can none the less contribute to financial flows into a region. Invisible earners such as banks, insurance companies, shipping interests and headquarters in general can clearly contribute to regional income; and, although there is no doubt that their locational preferences work primarily in favour of leader regions, especially those based on national capitals, there is also scope for non-productive activities to benefit other regional economies. This is well demonstrated by the tourist industry. OECD *Economic Surveys*, for example, show that Greek tourist earnings were approximately equivalent to 40 per cent of visible export earnings in the late 1970s, the corresponding figures for Spain and Portugal being 25 per cent and 30 per cent. Although these are national figures it is clear that, especially in terms of employment and the multiplier effect, a high proportion of the benefit was felt in the relatively limited number of areas that have been highly developed for tourism.

With respect to industry, a major criticism of export-base theory employed in the context of cumulative causation is that it can imply that the distinction between export-earning and other industries is clear-cut. Some industries, it is true, display export orientation or regional orientation fairly clearly, but in many cases markets are both internal and external to the region. Measurement of this split between regional and other markets is admittedly difficult becuase of the problem of data availability, but measurement problems do not invalidate concepts. Moreover, the idea that many firms should be regarded as drawing their income simultaneously from regional and external sources can be given additional significance by introducing a temporal dimension. Regional systems are temporally dynamic, and it is important to consider how firms and industries serving mixed markets have developed this characteristic. Some may always have possessed it, but it is likely that for others it has evolved. In some instances the starting point may have been export orientation, with regional markets emerging later in response to increasing local prosperity or as a consequence of the development of local forward linkages. But it is probable that many examples of mixed-market enterprise will have developed from an initial state of regional orientation. In these cases it is possible to envisage a process involving a breakthrough to wider markets being achieved by the more thrusting firms.

Such breakthroughs, it may be noted, have been greatly facilitated by technological developments, especially those relating to transportation and the optimum size of manufacturing units. Outstanding improvements have been made in all aspects of transportation, but those with the widest implications for regional systems have been related to road networks and, especially, to national motorway systems and the European motorway network. When it is possible for freight to be driven between the major markets of northern France and West Germany in a day, the scope for forward-looking firms to abandon the restrictions of regional markets is self-evident. Less obvious is the significance of the relationship between optimum factory size and the development of markets external to a region. In many industries a trend of far-reaching importance has been for improved technology to lead to the development of larger and fewer production units able to take advantage of economies of scale. One outcome has been that in some regions surplus capacity has been used to develop, in conjunction with improvements in transportation, expanded regional exports. By incorporating this type of export-earning potential into export-base theory it is possible to meet the criticism that the theory assumes that external demand will always be the prime activator of export growth. With this alternative view the expansion of supply can be taken as a spur to export orientation, although a condition of supply-based exporting must be that external markets are sufficient for the process to succeed. If this is the case a regional economy may be regarded as a 'seedbed', and it is interesting that one trend in the European approach to regional economic restructuring has been the attempt to exploit the seedbed concept by adopting measures intended to assist relatively small firms to break through barriers preventing them tapping far larger external markets.

Financial 'Leakage' and Regional Economies

A further problem associated with export-base theory is that it encourages the assumption that the financial flows of overwhelming importance to a region are those directed inwards from outside. The centre–periphery model, it is true, envisages that the acceptance of Northern investment opportunities by Southern investors can be an important component in polarisation flows, but this recognition does not stress sufficiently the mobility of investment capital in modern financial systems. Money deposited at a branch of a nationally organised bank in one region becomes a basis for credit at any other place in the bank's area of operations; unit-trust schemes are able to gather funds widely yet invest them with a spatial bias dictated by the location patterns of attractive investment opportunities; and private pension funds, which are major sources of investment finance generated by postwar prosperity, can similarly achieve large-scale interregional capital flows in the search for safe but worthwhile returns. Payments of interest, dividends and pensions ensure, of course, that the financial flows are not simply unidirectional, but the fact remains that capital moved in these and similar ways may fuel growth activities in regions other than the 'donor' area. In addition, however, it is necessary to appreciate that opportunities for finance to 'leak' from all types of region are much more varied than even this elaborated aspect of the centre–periphery model would suggest. Consequently the following discussion of business investment strategy and of regional expenditure on imported commodities, services and labour supplies is included to counterbalance over-emphasis on the export-earnings approach.

It has been argued recently that the loss of potential investment capital from a region is intimately linked with the question of business organisation, particularly when an activity is only one element in a major company with headquarters, and therefore the decision-making function, located outside the region. External control of investment decisions is a phenomenon closely associated with the growth of multinational investment, and it has recently attracted considerable attention (Brooke, 1977; Commission of the European Communities, 1977b; Hamilton, 1976; Massey, 1979). But the same phenomenon can also be a consequence of intranational development trends, including the absorption of activities by means of the takeover process and the emergence of major national firms with widespread branch-plant investment (Leigh and North, 1978). Whatever the pathway leading to the external control of investment decisions, the potential problem for a regional economy is that profits generated by externally controlled activities may be credited to the headquarters rather than the locality. Given this possibility, growth arising from regional reinvestment must be a process that is far from automatic, for capital will be invested geographically according to external predictions of what will become profit-generating areas.

Quite apart from the question of the location of decision-making, given the complexity of modern industry it is clear that many activities with significant external markets are unlikely to satisfy all their demands for materials, equipment and supporting services within their home region, even if it is a highly developed leader region. Inevitably, therefore, a proportion of their backward linkages will be external to the regional economy. For example, an investigation by Frederiksson and Lindmark (1979) in Sweden, which involved a sample survey of a very wide range of industries, concluded that one firm in twenty was directly involved in Volvo's subcontracting system and that, through a second round of linkages, one firm in twelve was indirectly associated with the firm. Far from being spatially concentrated, however, linked activities were identified in regions spread throughout much of the country. Thinking in cumulative causation terms, in this situation the stimulation of regional business in the 'home' region will fall below the theoretical maximum, and the multiplier effect of the personal demand chain will be weakened as potential income leaks away to the benefit of other regions. Similar effects may be expected from residentiary production since there is no reason to suppose that this will be able to satisfy all its functional requirements within the region. Moreover, a brief excursion through a typical department store or supermarket is sufficient to underline the extent to which residentiary industries normally cover only a fraction of the range of goods demanded by Europeans in the late twentieth century. In this instance it is true that the absence of regional production creates employment in the wholesaling, retailing and transport spheres, yet employment based on procurement is unlikely to equal that based on production; and in any case there are some forms of demand, such as that for tourism, which it may be impossible to satisfy by means of regional imports. Consequently, the lack of comprehensive residentiary production, a characteristic and very striking feature of modern regional economies, may also be seen as an important source of leakage capable of reducing significantly the overall impact of total regional earnings.

Hard and fast rules concerning the scale of this form of leakage are impossible to establish, primarily because import flow is a variable controlled by other complex variables, such as a region's size and the details of its economic structure. However, broad indications of the importance of external purchasing, in comparison with internal movements and regional exports, can be given. Data for the Dutch standard regions, for example, indicate that imports are equivalent to a third of the commodity movements within the North Region, whereas the corresponding proportion for exports is a quarter. The South, a major industrial region including the headquarters and many satellites of the Philips empire, records imports equivalent to 27 per cent of internal movements, compared with an export figure of 45 per cent.

While leakage from regional economies is to a great extent a function of the need to obtain and pay for a very wide range of commodities, the phenomenon is also apparent in the working of the labour market. A characteristic of regions throughout the Community, but especially those enjoying the greatest prosperity, is that their major employment centres cannot satisfy their labour demands in the immediate locality. The typical outcome is that labour is imported by demand centres, in most instances with little effect on a region's financial system since the dominant flow is likely to be intraregional commuting. But it is not uncommon for labour to be imported in significant quantities, as is often the case with regions lying close to national frontiers (Commission of the European Communities, forthcoming). As with the movement of commodities, international commuting can work both ways, but conditions on either side of a frontier may be so contrasted that the flow is primarily unidirectional, with the result that the scale of leakage is fairly clear. Tuppen (1978) has drawn attention to the West German and Swiss economies as generators of international commuting, while Burtenshaw (1976b) has examined the West German Saarland. In the mid-1970s the predominant international flow of more than 15,000 workers was from France into the Saarland, with the latter also generating a net inflow of 8,000 from neighbouring parts of West Germany. While it is true that the Saarland benefited by achieving a higher level of development than would otherwise have been possible, and while it should not be assumed that all the migrants occupied highly remunerative jobs, the fact remains that the number of workers exporting virtually all their income from the region was equivalent to the labour force of a major car factory. What is also noteworthy is that this example and Tuppen's work illustrate the temporal dynamism often associated with this type of regional financial leakage. Between the mid-1960s and the mid-1970s the Saarland virtually tripled its labour intake from France, while the number of workers from Alsace employed in the West German and Swiss economies similarly rose from 10,000 in 1964 to 27,000 in 1976. But it can be anticipated that in the late 1970s intensifying recessional conditions affected very severely the commuting flows to these and other regions.

Transfrontier commuting, however, is not the sole form of labour movement able to influence significantly the flow of finance from a region (King, 1976; Salt and Clout, 1976; Paine, 1977). This is graphically shown by the case of West Germany. Mediterranean 'guest' workers drawn into principal employment centres in this country accounted for a tenth of the national labour force in the mid-1970s; Hessen, Nordrhein-Westfalen and Südbayern all recorded figures well above this average, and in Baden-Würtenburg the proportion was no less than a quarter. Since these migrants resided in the regions in which they were employed it must be acknowledged that their demand effects contributed to growth via the multiplier; and, as with transfrontier commuting, the presence of the migrants was instrumental in achieving higher development levels. But because an important aim of the migrants was to support relatives in their home country by means of remittances, the scope for leakage was clearly substantial and, it may be noted, was closely related to the concept of trickling down.

From this survey of the leakage phenomenon it is apparent that the channels through which finance can escape from a regional economy are by no means negligible. Leakage must be seen as a counterflow to export earnings, and a regional economy can be conceptualised as an open financial system inextricably linked with similar systems by means of complex inward and outward flows.

Because all regions experience these two-way movements, however, the extent to which a region will be hampered by leakage will depend to a considerable extent on its ability to compensate by exploiting, in the form of export earnings, the deficiencies of other areas. Regions performing well in this respect will be the net beneficiaries of financial polarisation; those that are less successful will become its victims. This observation must form a backdrop to any consideration of regional development strategies but, before attention turns to these strategies, one further dimension of the Community's regional economies must be examined – the working of the public sector. Public involvement across a rapidly broadening front has been a key feature of the postwar period and, although many policies have been conceived at the national level, their implementation has frequently had regional economic consequences. The significance of the public sector at the regional level was at least partially recognised by Myrdal and incorporated into his cumulative causation model but, with a few exceptions, subsequent attention given to this subject has been regrettably slight.

Regional Economies and the Public Sector

In some respects the activities of the public sector are, or are intended to be, akin to those of private enterprise. This is particularly the case with nationalised or partly nationalised industries, which are of widespread importance (Holland, 1972; Maunder, 1979; Sheahan, 1976; Streit, 1977). Various arguments are advanced in favour of nationalisation, such as the necessity to remove control of vital industries from capitalist decision-makers, the responsibility to ensure that fundamental growth activities evolve in a coherent and efficient manner and the desirability of procuring for society in general the profitability of activities with long-term growth potential. Whatever the motives, however, historically there has been an assumption that nationalised activities can be run on a profitable basis, in which case the consequences for regional economies should not differ markedly from those anticipated under private enterprise.

Despite the British predisposition to equate loss-making with nationalisation, profitable examples of public ownership are not uncommon in the Community, and the parallel with private enterprise must therefore be at least partially accepted. Yet the fact remains that state ownership is also associated with accumulation of losses, sometimes well beyond the funding capacity of private firms. Indeed, as the state takeover of British Leyland demonstrates, in the late twentieth century large-scale losses and the threat of industrial collapse can be the instigators of nationalisation. In effect, state funding of major deficits acts as a subsidy to the regions in which the loss-making enterprises are located and, depending on the nature of the enterprise, subsidisation may be widespread or concentrated. Heavy subsidisation of rail networks is, for example, common throughout the Community, whereas support for loss-making car plants or steelworks is necessarily restricted to a minority of European regions. From an individual region's viewpoint, however, the spatial dimension of subsidisation is less important than the temporal dimension, for the question of real significance is the length of time that subsidisation of losses within the region will be tolerated.

In many cases the fact that loss-making activities have been under state control has retarded the evolutionary process that might be expected to operate within the affected regional economies under private enterprise. In some instances this has probably been a desirable development. Partial state involvement in the Dutch coal industry was instrumental in achieving an orderly retreat from mining in the late 1960s and early 1970s (Pinder, 1976); more positively, French intervention in Renault has been associated with the emergence of highly competitive products – in 1980 Renault was one of the few profitable major car manufacturers. Conversely, however, political considerations leading to failure to rationalise and adopt forward-looking policies can be counter-productive, especially if this failure is maintained for a lengthy period. In this circumstance regional communities and economies may eventually face sudden, far-reaching changes as policies are revised and important activities are cut back. Furthermore, as British Steel's recent history demonstrates, one unwelcome consequence of delay may be the concentration of contraction into a period in which it may be extremely difficult to attract to an affected region alternative investment to maintain cumulative causation and multiplier effects.

Discussion of subsidies for loss-making nationalised activities leads to the general question of the funding of public expenditure. Finance available to public authorities at all levels is, of course, primarily accumulated via the taxation systems, with personal, business and value-added taxes acting as the most prominent sources of income. Through these channels the populations and business communities of all regions make major contributions to their respective national exchequers, so that each regional economy is subject to this additional and substantial type of leakage, the immediate effect of which is a reduction in the gross demand available locally. Government spending naturally returns taxation to the regional economies, the returned finance frequently being supplemented by public sector borrowing; but when all forms of expenditure are taken into account a particular region may receive more or less than its 'fair' share. As Law (1975) and Bennett (1980) have stressed, calculation of the balance between regional taxation and public expenditure is a complex and controversial issue, and it has yet to be thoroughly investigated in the Community, although the MacDougall Report (Commission of the European Communities, 1977c) is an important first step in this direction. What is clear is that broad spatial variations in the taxation/expenditure relationship can be identified, even though the precise nature of these variations is open to question. For example, in considering the financial implications of independence for Northern Ireland, Scotland and Wales, Law tentatively concluded that the loss of financial support from England would require all three breakaway areas to find additional income of approximately £80–£90 per capita at late-1960s prices. But much detailed work remains to be done in this field and, although for any region the issue might crudely be said to be a matter of net gain or loss, consideration must also be given to the channels through which taxation and public loans are redistributed, for these influence the scale and type of demand returned to each regional economy.

A major outlet for public expenditure is the creation of direct employment. In Britain, for example, there were slightly more than 5 million employees of central and local government in the late 1970s; this was two and a half times the labour force of the nationalised corporations, as well as being equivalent to a fifth of employment in the country as a whole (HMSO, 1980). So far as regions are concerned, a significant feature of this direct employment is that in all advanced countries a large majority of it is spatially well distributed. For example, work for teachers, the police, health service employees, planners and administrators is roughly generated according to the size of regional populations. The result is that in all regions a substantial proportion of the personal demand which feeds the multiplier mechanism can be attributed to this source. Furthermore, direct employment has recently grown rapidly in all Community countries (in Britain the expansion between 1961 and 1978 was no less than 40 per cent) and it can therefore be concluded that an important expanding feature of most regional economies has been the contribution of public employment to the personal demand chain. However, by no means all the direct employment is spatially well distributed. Central government, it is true, requires many regional offices and agencies but, given the administrative systems prevalent in the Community today, it is inevitable that capital regions account for disproportionate shares of the central administrative system. For these regions the administrative function assumes a significance very similar to that of private sector export-earning activities: administrative services are provided for the country as a whole and, in exchange, tax contributions are drawn in and stimulate the regional economy. Similarly with defence, employment in the armed forces is normally concentrated rather than evenly spread and, as Riley and Smith (1981) have shown, although military bases may not dominate entire regional economies, their income can be of great importance in the generation of sub-regional multiplier effects. Equally, however, the presence of major defence establishments may inhibit the expected evolution of the cumulative causation process. Their linkages, for example, are likely to lie outside the region, while their domination of the local labour market may stifle local enterprise and the emergence of more normal economic structures, dangers also associated with the presence of monolithic private sector employers.

A quite different channel through which public expenditure produces a regional economic impact is its demand effect on the private sector, the breadth of which has been stressed by Rees (1973) in a brief but revealing discussion. Consideration of the purchasing requirements of central and local government once again leads to the conclusion that, depending on the specific circumstances, the regional stimuli may be both well distributed and concentrated. Day-to-day requirements are so varied and commonplace that dispersed regional purchasing may be anticipated. Indeed, at least in the British case a policy of purchasing throughout the development areas has been pursued. Similarly infrastructure expenditure, an essential stimulant for large parts of the construction industry, produces widespread injections to regional economies as public stocks of housing, educational, health, energy and transport facilities are increased. But in other instances the spatial impact is necessarily restricted, at least initially. Modern defence equipment, for example, is in general the product of high-technology activities such as the aerospace and electronics industries, which are far from evenly spread through the West European regional system. Likewise the production of advanced medical equipment is in the hands of a limited number of producers. Yet it must be remembered that firms in industries of this type are often assemblers of an extensive range of components produced by branch plants or independent suppliers and, in either case, more widespread regional stimuli may be anticipated. Branches are commonly located outside a company's home region and, although some component suppliers conform with the cumulative causation model by locating close to their major customers, in many instances the high value of their products undermines the necessity for proximity. So does the fact that most suppliers are linked with a number of consumers rather than a single dominant one. While the overall picture is far from fully researched, therefore, it seems likely that many regions ultimately gain some benefit from public high-technology expenditure that is initially concentrated.

The remaining major opportunity for public finance to be returned to regional economies is by means of the social security system. Rudimentary provision for social assistance has been made by some European countries since well before the Second World War; contributory, but state-subsidised old age and disability pension schemes were founded in Germany in 1889, while in Britain the Old Age Pensions Act came into force in 1908, to be followed three years later by the first National Insurance Act. Yet the Community's present-day social security systems are a far cry from the early experiments, as work by Lawson and Reed (1975) and Maynard (1975) underlines. In most member states in the 1970s the proportion of national income devoted to assistance was between 20 and 30 per cent, and during the 1960s and 1970s there was a strong tendency for per capita social security expenditure to rise. For example, after allowing for inflation, in West Germany, France and Italy per capita expenditure rose by a factor of approximately 2·5 between 1962 and 1977, while in Belgium the increase was threefold and in the Netherlands almost fourfold (Table 3.1). Social security is paid as cash benefits and it is therefore clear that its scope for contributing to multiplier effects by maintaining demand among society's disadvantaged groups has become considerable. What must be examined, however, is its propensity to differentiate between regions, supporting some disproportionately by the positive transfer of resources.

It is apparent that some benefits account for too small a proportion of total expenditure to be capable of distorting the overall resource flow in favour of a restricted number of regions. As Table 3.2 reveals, family allowances and insurance for industrial injuries both typically account for a small fraction of all social security payments. Two other forms of benefit,

Table 3.1   *Social Protection Expenditure by Community Members*

	Index of per capita expenditure at 1970 prices (1970 = 100)		Social protection as % of GDP		
	1962	1977	1962	1977	Change
West Germany	63	152	19·4	27·4	+ 8·0
France	60	156	16·6	23·9	+ 7·3
Italy	49	139	14·3	23·1	+ 8·8
Netherlands	45	169	14·1	28·8	+14·7
Belgium	59	174	15·8	26·2	+10·4
Luxembourg	61	168	14·9	25·8	+10·9
United Kingdom	—	138	16·3[b]	19·7	+ 3·4
Ireland	—	171[a]	13·2[b]	19·2[a]	+ 6·0
Denmark	—	156	19·5[b]	25·4	+ 5·9

Notes: a   1976 figure.   b   1970 figure.
Source: Commission of the European Communities, 1980b, p. 105.

general health insurance and pension rights, are quantitatively of much greater importance: throughout the Community between 23 and 30 per cent of all assistance took the form of sickness benefit in the late 1970s, while the proportion absorbed by state pensions was between 28 and 45 per cent. Particularly in the case of pensions an element of regional bias may be hypothesised: ageing population structures are typical of many lagging regions that have experienced out-migration among people of working age, and the phenomenon of favoured retirement regions is also well known. Even so, very substantial biases in regional pension receipts cannot be assumed, primarily because the migration factor will in general modify, rather than fundamentally change, the proportional importance of a region's pensionable population. Finally, although unemployment benefit is by definition biased in favour of regions experiencing relatively weak economic momentum, it is again arguable that income via this channel is significant for all, rather than a few, regions. As the current experience of all Community members demonstrates, unemployment is a ubiquitous phenomenon whose regional variation is a matter of degree.

Taking a broad view, therefore, it appears that today's

Table 3.2 The Structure of Social Protection Benefits in Community Members, 1977

	West Germany	France	Italy	Netherlands	Belgium	Luxembourg	United Kingdom	Ireland[a]	Denmark
	Percentage share of all social protection expenditure								
Sickness benefit	29·0	26·7	26·4	29·7	25·3	23·3	25·8	35·2	29·3
Long-term invalidity benefit	7·9	5·7	20·6	18·3[b]	7·1	8·7	8·9	5·4	10·4
Occupational illness benefit	3·4	3·9	2·6	—	3·8	5·6	0·9	0·6	0·8
Old age pensions	28·7	37·0	30·5	30·6	37·4[c]	37·3	43·8	33·2[c]	31·3
Widows' pensions, etc.	15·8	5·9	6·3	5·4	—	14·9	2·8	—	0·6
Family allowances and maternity benefit	9·1	14·8	9·0	10·1	14·0	9·4	10·7	13·4	11·3
Unemployment benefit	2·5	4·3	2·3	5·5	8·1	0·3	5·8	10·2	12·5
Other benefits	3·6	1·7	2·3	0·4	4·3	0·5	1·3	2·0	3·8
	100·0	100·0	100·0	100·0	100·0	100·0	100·0	100·0	100·0

Notes: a 1976 figures. b Including occupational illness benefit. c Including widows' pensions, etc.
Source: Commission of the European Communities, 1980b, pp. 108–9.

comprehensive social security systems are an important form of income for all regions, and it is against this background that their significance must be considered. Within the regional system, social security mechanisms generally achieve a transfer of resources in favour of low income groups or those whose income is threatened by illness or unemployment. For individuals this transfer may be critical for the maintenance of living standards, and if the effects on individuals are aggregated the outcome for a region is that basic demand levels are sustained and protected, with obvious implications for the regional multiplier. Social security is therefore a force contributing to stability in regional economies, a force to which we shall return when considering progress in regional development in Chapter 5.

Before leaving the question of public expenditure it is constructive to compare the preceding interpretation of the role of the public sector with conclusions that may be drawn from Short's (1978) investigation of the distribution of public sector spending in Britain. Focusing on the period 1969–74, and considering expenditure on a per capita basis, Short's main finding was that 'quite striking variations existed between regions . . . Scotland had almost 40 per cent more expenditure than the lowest region – the West Midlands'. At first sight this weakens the argument that the public sector's impact is of widespread fundamental significance, an impression created by Short's emphasis on the most extreme regions – those with the highest and lowest per capita spending. But if consideration is given to all regions, and in particular to the relationships between their per capita expenditure figures and the national average, the argument is in fact supported.

Table 3.3 demonstrates this by presenting the core of Short's data distilled into the statistical index known as the coefficient of variation. For each type of policy, source of expenditure and type of expenditure a mean value for per capita spending in all regions has been calculated; the deviations of individual regional figures from the means have been processed to provide the statistical measure known as the standard deviation; and, finally, coefficients of variation have been derived by expressing the standard deviations as percentages of their respective means. The interpretation of the results is straightforward: small coefficients indicate that the data are

Table 3.3 *Reanalysis of Short's (1978) Data for Public Expenditure in British Standard Regions*

	% of total expenditure	Coefficient of variation between regions (%)
A: Expenditure by policy		
Agriculture, fisheries and food	2·1	54·1
Trade, industry and employment	6·2	44·3
Nationalised industries' capital expenditure	8·3	26·4
Roads and transport	5·7	19·8
Housing	9·7	31·3
Other environmental services	6·7	11·5
Law, order and protective services	3·4	12·6
Education, libraries, science and arts	17·6	8·3
Health, personal services	14·8	9·1
Social security	25·5	8·7
	100·0	11·5
B: Source of expenditure		
Central government	53·5	12·2
Local government	35·9	11·8
Public corporations	10·6	20·9
	100·0	11·5
C: Type of expenditure		
Current	69·3	8·8
Capital	30·7	18·2
	100·0	11·5

Coefficient of variation $= \dfrac{\sigma}{\bar{x}} = \dfrac{\text{standard deviation of all regional values}}{\text{mean of all regional values}}$

Standard deviation $= \sqrt{\dfrac{\Sigma(x - \bar{x})^2}{n}}$ where $\bar{x}$ is the mean for all regions, x is an individual regional observation and n is the number of regions. Σ is a summation sign.

Source of original data: Short, 1978, p. 503.

clustered around the mean and that regional contrasts are muted; large coefficients signify the reverse. From section A of Table 3.3 it is apparent that expenditure under the first five policy headings produced large coefficients (19–54 per cent). Regional contrasts in per capita spending under these headings must be considered substantial, but to some extent this group of results is little more than might be expected. Nationalised industries are not evenly distributed throughout the British regional system; the heading trade, industry and employment includes expenditure incurred in the context of regional policy; and, when a short time period such as this one is studied, road programmes are likely to affect some regions much more than others.

While these large coefficients were to some extent predictable, Table 3.3 also demonstrates that the policies with which they were associated were by no means dominant: altogether this group absorbed only a third of public expenditure in the mid-1970s. In contrast, the remaining two-thirds were accounted for by policies recording coefficients of less than 13 per cent, and in three instances coefficients of less than 10 per cent were associated with particularly large shares of total expenditure (15–26 per cent). In addition, three other features of the table deserve attention. The first is that total spending, the sum of expenditure under all policy headings, also produced a relatively small coefficient (11·5 per cent). Secondly, the only expenditure source in section B to record a moderately large coefficient was that of the public corporations, which accounted for only a tenth of all spending. Thirdly, current expenditure (wage bills and recurring purchases) absorbed more than two-thirds of the finance, yet produced one of the lowest coefficients in the entire analysis. Viewing these results as a whole, therefore, the picture which emerges is that, although regional variations in the incidence of public expenditure cannot be ignored, the state's spending power is undeniably a major influence throughout the British regional system. Because other economically advanced countries have experienced similar public sector growth in the postwar period, it seems that this general conclusion has much wider validity in the European Community.

Chapters 2 and 3 have examined a range of theories offering

deeper insights into the processes which allow some areas to prosper while others languish or decline. They have also sought to demonstrate that regional economies are extremely intricate, are subject to constant evolution and are essentially open systems inextricably connected with each other. Ideally, intervention policies designed to solve specific regional economic problems should be designed with this complexity in mind. Whether this has in fact happened is a moot point, but there has been no shortage of intervention packages intended to correct the paths followed by individual regions or entire regional systems. At this point, therefore, we move on to examine regional economic planning as practised in individual Community countries and in the Community as a whole.

4 *Strategies for Regional Industrialisation*

It was suggested in Chaper 1 that the desire to prevent the re-emergence of unemployment, hardship and poverty on the scale experienced in the 1930s was a prime stimulant to economic planning in the immediate postwar era. This planning had two interrelated facets: at the macroeconomic level national planning intended to achieve controlled, yet continuing, growth rapidly became the vogue (Aldcroft, 1978), while policies designed to steer this growth into problem regions emerged and became increasingly well defined. To some extent these policies attempted to work by promoting the development of non-manufacturing activities, especially agriculture and the tourist industry. However, largely because of problems of seasonality and, in the case of agriculture, limited employment creation, involvement in these activities has been subsidiary to policies based on industrial promotion. This chapter therefore focuses on the emphasis given to industrialisation, and to the creation of conditions thought to be conducive to industrialisation, throughout the postwar period.

National Strategies

Yuill, Allen and Hull (1980) have provided a comprehensive, well-illustrated survey of the evolution of regional policy in Community member countries and it is therefore unnecessary to consider each country in detail here. What must be stressed is the proliferation that took place in the regional policy field as the principle of intervention in regional economic processes became established. In the early 1950s restricted industrial problem regions or pockets of rural backwardness were generally considered to be prime targets for assistance (the chief exception to this being the case of southern Italy) and there was optimism that rapid change would be achieved in these areas as growth from Europe's resurgent industrial base was partially channelled to their benefit. It soon became apparent, however, that early predictions of rapid economic restructuring were over-optimistic and, as the time scale for intervention was lengthened, changing attitudes and economic circumstances brought about much more liberal approaches to the definition of development areas. Broad 'peripheral' problem regions suffering population expulsion were defined; from the late 1950s onwards, aid to declining coalfields became commonplace as the industry adjusted to the rapid erosion of its markets by oil (Gordon, 1970); and the substitution of capital for labour, coupled with the effects of growing foreign competition, prepared the way for the extension of assistance to many industrial centres that had flourished on former growth-pole activities. Once established, few development areas have lost that status, although Britain's recent curtailment of them is an obvious exception. By the early 1980s, therefore, only the Netherlands had less than 20 per cent of its population in assisted regions, the norm (as exemplified by France, West Germany, Ireland and Italy) was approximately 35 per cent and in Belgium the figure was no less than 42 per cent.

At this point several observations are relevant to the relationships between theory and regional development problems and policies. Although the strong emphasis on steering mobile industrial investment to development areas is most obviously connected with the desire to fulfil promises of job creation in high-unemployment areas, because this investment does not normally serve regional markets it possesses the added attraction of regional export-earning potential. Similarly, export-base theory has lain behind attempts to encourage industries already present in problem regions to expand by means of more effective exploitation of external markets. Improvements in the cumulative causation process have been anticipated on the grounds that new multiplier effects will elevate the aggregate level of personal demand; and, associated with this idea, it has been pointed out that high-wage industries are able to bring particularly valuable stimuli to problem regions. In this connection the steel, car, electronics, oil-refining and petro-chemical industries have been given special attention, the implantation of branches of these industries in development areas having been a well-recognised facet of regional policy implementation. In addition to stimulating the personal-demand multiplier through high wages, however, it has been argued that these implanted industries should contribute to cumulative causation because of their linkage effects. Here the early assumption was that significant local linkages with exist-ing and new firms might be generated because the implanted activities were branches of leading industries functioning as propulsive activities in late-twentieth-century growth poles. Retrospectively, however, it has become apparent that growth poles existing in economic space need no longer give rise to strong geographical concentrations of associated firms, a mis-match between theory and reality to which we shall return when considering the European Investment Bank's activities.

In addition to these links with economic theory, several connections with aspects of behaviour and perception may be identified. For example, governments opting for spatial equilibrium policies have assumed, explicitly or implicitly, that behavioural and perception constraints have prevented many industrial decision-makers from achieving truly objec-tive analyses of interregional investment opportunities. In contrast, policy-makers have presented themselves as posses-sing spatially unbiased views which give rise to an appreciation of the sub-optimal resource use characteristic of regional sys-tems in disequilibrium. As a result, regional policies have been marketed as rational attempts to acheive improved utilisation of labour, capital and other resources by correcting the inaccu-rate mental maps possessed by industrial decision-makers. But although these policies may be presented as strategies designed to mould the wayward behaviour of the industrial investor and encourage Hirschman's 'special kind of bold-ness', the fact that governments are groups of politically moti-vated individuals whose viewpoints and actions are strongly influenced by their outlook on society cannot be disregarded. Politicians' perceptions are pitted against investors' percep-tions; beneath the surface, regional policies are not entirely divorced from pressures emanating from apparently separate government policies; and, as one political party or coalition is forced to relinquish power to another, shifts of emphasis or orientation in regional policy frequently occur.

Almost irrespective of the actual size of Community member countries, the problem of overcoming handicaps arising from remoteness has become a long-running regional policy theme which may also be related to behavioural theory. In the heart of the Community, for example, the regional policies of Belgium and the Netherlands assume the influence of a remoteness factor in the southern Ardennes and in the Dutch North, even though the most remote parts of these regions lie within a radius of 200 km of the heart of their respective leader regions (Riley, 1976; Pinder, 1976; Thoman, 1973). This phenomenon has yet to be fully investigated, but it may be that this particular policy feature is a response to the tendency of individuals to perceive distances within the national space in relative, rather than absolute, terms. Even in small countries a relative view of the national space could cultivate the belief that certain regions are distant, an assumption from which industrial decision-makers would be unlikely to be entirely immune.

Recognition of the remoteness factor contributed to a wider appreciation of the centre–periphery model and to regional policy expansion up to the late 1960s. Within individual countries, leader regions were considered to be increasingly congested centres exerting costly polarising forces throughout the national space (Eversley, 1972; Pinder, 1981); it was concluded that natural trickling down was generally ineffective compared with polarisation; and the designation of development areas therefore became a cornerstone of attempts to stimulate artificially the trickling-down process. While central governments have stressed the need for balanced development in entire regional systems, however, planners in the problem regions have understandably remained preoccupied with the promotion of local interests. For the regional economic planner in the front line, every success in generating additional employment in his region is a visible step forward, and every industrialist attracted by another region is a lost opportunity. Faced with the reality of interregional competition, planners and local politicians frequently regard the task of regional promotion as a marketing exercise (Camina, 1974). Advertisements in the national press for regions and for specific localities are one familiar facet of this approach (Mason, 1981); the distribution of highly professional publicity material is another; from time to time there may be intensive promotional campaigns; and delegations from major regions or industrial centres may make international tours. All this, of course, is designed to achieve wider awareness of, and interest in, the region in question. The aim is nothing less than to remould in a favourable manner the decision-maker's perception of the region.

At the national level, where there is a greater tendency to take an overall view, a well-recognised policy option is to restrain the growth of leader regions (Emanuel, 1973). Obvious though this may seem, however, it is an option that has not proved popular. The principal exception to this rule is the British Industrial Development Certificate (IDC) system, which dates from the Town and Country Planning Act of 1947 and was supplemented by the introduction of Office Development Permits in the mid-1960s. Apart from this only one other restraint system (for Paris in 1955) emerged before 1970, since when only two others (for Italy and the Netherlands) have been introduced (Jarrett, 1975). Thus, despite the realisation that disequilibrium is fuelled by the attractive power of some regions, as well as by the weaknesses of others, the tools selected to engender greater equilibrium have concentrated on drawing growth to development areas rather than on expelling it from leader regions or on blocking its gravitation to them.

OBSTACLES TO LEADER-REGION RESTRAINT

One reason why restraint systems have not become widespread is that there is disagreement over the form that restraint should take. While some proponents of restrictions have argued that they should be exercised over all construction, as was originally proposed for the highly congested western Netherlands, others have pressed the case for limiting control to the secondary and tertiary economic sectors (as has been done in France and Britain). But control may also be limited to the secondary sector (the Italian system) and, even when the question of sectoral emphasis has been resolved, the list of fundamental policy decisions to be taken remains significant. For example, the machinery for control may be made applicable only in leader regions. Alternatively, as was long the case in Britain, it can be made a nationwide system, with permission for developments in assisted areas normally being little more than a formality, and with policy formulators enjoying a measure of discretion as to the severity with which controls are applied throughout the rest of the regional system. With respect to the scale of developments it is necessary to decide whether investors must obtain permission only if their projects exceed a certain threshold size. If so, should the threshold be defined in terms of investment, floorspace, or employment? And should restraint be exercised through a licensing system or, as was originally intended in the Dutch experiment, by means of a tax analogous to a fine imposed for fuelling leader-region congestion?

Although allowing room for much disagreement and delay, these practical issues imply that restraint is a desirable goal. But movement towards this goal has undoubtedly been hindered by the fact that agreement on the desirability of restraint is far from unanimous. It seems very probable that more widespread control has been obstructed by pressures brought to bear on policy-makers by the private sector, and there is no doubt that policy-makers are themselves divided over the wisdom of control. In this connection an important consideration has been that development that is blocked in one locality is not automatically destined for development areas. Investors may abandon their plans completely or modify them to comply with leader-region restrictions. Another possibility is that they may divert to regions outside the development areas where little or no control is exercised. And, especially when multinational investment is involved, there is a danger that investment will be channelled to more liberal Community countries, which may see their absence of restraint as a competitive advantage.

Opposition to restraint must also be explained in temporal terms. Support for the concept was greatest during the Community's postwar industrial upswing, when there were marked labour shortages in leader regions and when industrialists' optimism, coupled with demand for labour and land, led to more open-minded attitudes to non-central locations.

With the onset and intensification of recession in the 1970s much of this support evaporated as slack labour markets reappeared and as investment was curtailed. Confidence in regional restraint has certainly declined as leader-region planners have recently begun the process of adjustment to the problems of achieving satisfactory local growth rates, a change of attitude that is now finding expression in policy modifications (Nicol, 1979). Britain's IDC system has been diluted so that industrial developments of less than 4,650 square metres are no longer subject to control in the South East, control in the Paris region has been relaxed somewhat since 1973–4 and the Dutch government has suggested that the western Netherlands' development tax (which has never been fully operational because of the recession) should be abolished.

REGIONAL INDUSTRIALISATION INCENTIVES

In sharp contrast to restraint systems, there has been a proliferation of incentives intended to promote the regional industrialisation process. These incentives involve the transfer of resources from the public purse to the private sector, and it is therefore hardly surprising that Community members have attempted to ensure that projects conform with certain conditions before they become eligible for aid. As with many aspects of the incentive phenomenon, these conditions vary from country to country, but several recurrent themes can be identified. One is that projects have commonly been required to conform with any physical planning strategy operating in the area chosen for investment. A second, more recent, trend has been increasing emphasis on the requirement that developments should be environmentally benign. Thirdly, stress has been placed on attempting to ensure that assisted projects are economically viable; and, since viability may mean profit for a firm yet almost no local benefit, it has been necessary for would-be recipients of aid to demonstrate that a project is likely to have a favourable impact on the host region. 'Favourable impact' can, of course, be related in a variety of ways to the economic theories examined earlier but, so far as the general public is concerned, the most prominent justification has been the employment to be created by proposed developments. In view of the relationship between unemployment and the rise of regional policies the political logic behind this is obvious, and potential investors have been quick to appreciate that subsidies for their schemes are easier to obtain if the favourable implications for the labour market are stressed.

Assuming that a project conforms with a general set of requirements, what will the investor be offered by way of inducement to put the plan into practice? Detailed surveys by Emanuel (1973), Thoman (1973), the Commission of the European Communities (1979b), Vanhove and Klaassen (1980) and Yuill, Allen and Hull (1980) demonstrate that the range of incentives is extremely wide and complex. The Yuill, Allen and Hull study, for example, identified no less than twenty-five substantial inducements offered by Community members, each backed by conditions and operational formulas that varied markedly from country to country. Despite this complexity the incentives currently available can be divided into five broad categories: labour subsidies, depreciation allowances, tax concessions, interest-related subsidies and capital grants. From Table 4.1, which shows the incidence of these categories throughout the Nine, it is immediately apparent that the approach adopted by most countries has been to market a package of inducements instead of relying on a single

Table 4.1 *Principal Regional Incentives*

	Capital grant	Interest-related subsidy	Tax concession	Depreciation allowance	Labour subsidy
Belgium		○ ○^{a}		○	
Denmark	○	○ ○			
France	●		●		
West Germany	● ○		●		●
Ireland	○ ○		●		
Italy	●	●	●		●
Luxembourg	○			○	
Netherlands	◓				
United Kingdom	● ○	○^{a}			

Key: ○ discretionary incentive; ● automatic incentive; ◓ semi-automatic incentive (discretion chiefly associated with major projects).
Note: a Capital grants calculable as soft-loan incentives.
Source: Compiled from Yuill, Allen and Hull, 1980, tables 11.3 and 11.4.

measure. Here the underlying philosophy is clear: if one form of assistance fails to appeal another may succeed, and in some instances the attractions of individual incentives may reinforce each other in a cumulative fashion to overwhelm the decision-maker's uncertainty.

Green (1977) has concluded that in this respect the packages offered can be remarkably inefficient because of entrepreneurs' ignorance of them. In addition there is the paradox that some incentives may actually create uncertainty because they are available on a discretionary, rather than an automatic, basis. From a government's viewpoint the discretionary system may be readily justified: oversubsidisation can be lessened, thereby saving public money, and the assistance offered can be scaled to match the project's likely contribution to regional restructuring. But the entrepreneur is faced with the task of finding the formula that will present his project to the best advantage, and the reality is that in many instances he must ultimately decide whether to accept a subsidy falling short of the widely publicised ceiling figure to which he was originally attracted.

Although it is a relatively straightforward matter to rationalise the Community members' incentive measures into packages, their comparative evaluation is an exercise fraught with difficulty. The incentive mix varies from country to country, the discretionary element is a major variable and the potential value of a package for an individual firm is strongly dependent on factors such as its funding requirements, its profitability and the prevailing interest rates. Moreover, comparison can be complicated by the differential application of incentives within development areas. Instead of allowing blanket coverage there have been attempts (primarily by Italy, West Germany, Britain, the Netherlands and Belgium) to steer investment within the development areas by varying the maximum value of the packages according to the severity of regional problems. And, in similar vein, some incentives can only be obtained by investing in priority areas (such as the Danish Special Development Regions) within the development area system.

Because of this broad spectrum of complicating factors, even the most seasoned regional policy observers are reluctant to rank the packages available in Community member countries. With respect to spatial availability, Yuill, Allen and Hull (1980) are only prepared to identify the Irish and Italian measures as being particularly generous, with the Danish scheme (and possibly those of the Netherlands and West Germany) being relatively restrictive. Turning to the degree of subsidisation offered, the same authors again identify the measures available in Italy and Ireland (including Northern Ireland) as being the most valuable; but they are not prepared to differentiate between the remainder of the Nine, except to observe that Britain may be slightly more generous, and Luxembourg slightly less generous, than the norm. These conclusions may simply indicate that most Community countries have independently reached similar viewpoints as to the effort that is required, or can be afforded, to guide their regional systems towards more balanced development. But another interpretation is that, especially with respect to mobile foreign investment, individual members have found it necessary to ensure that their incentive packages are not at a competitive disadvantage relative to those of neighbouring countries. This interpretation has been explored by Emanuel (1973), who has underlined the danger of the process leading to 'competitive overbidding' (p. 158):

> Regional incentives . . . may . . . have the unintended effect of giving foreign investors a bonus which may not be required . . . The more that countries compete among themselves in the matter of incentives the larger and more costly the bonus . . .

Emanuel has called for international co-operation to limit unnecessary competition, and his call has been echoed by the European Commission in its attempts to achieve what is considered to be a more realistic spatial match between need and investment (Commission of the European Communities, 1976). But Emanuel has also stressed that, although incentives are a very obvious form of assistance, they are not the sole vehicle for regional policy. Despite the publicity given to incentive schemes in the postwar period, the amount that has actually been spent on these packages has been outstripped by investments in regional infrastructure. Sometimes these investments have been part of national programmes covering healthy as well as lagging regions; sometimes they have been limited to development areas; but in all cases the regional policy justification underlying the expenditure has been that it produces a marked improvement in the framework of facilities and services necessary to ensure the efficient operation of existing and future developments.

Infrastructure investments are often considered under two headings: economic overhead capital (EOC) and social overhead capital (SOC). SOC expenditure, which includes health facilities, education provision, libraries and recreational facilities may not be of obvious relevance to regional economic problems. Partly for this reason, and partly because expenditure and impact are difficult to establish, the study of SOC policies has been widely neglected. Klaassen (1968) has strongly underlined their significance, however, and it is no accident that promotional material published by regional development agencies frequently highlights SOC provision. To quote just one example:

> Water-sports enthusiasts will find excellent facilities . . . in most centres there is a new indoor swimming pool and a modern hall for indoor sports . . . [and] open air pools, tennis courts and hockey clubs are to be found at all centres . . .
> (Economic Technological Institute for Drenthe)

Investment in EOC is of obvious direct relevance to the industrialisation process since this heading covers expenditure on roads, industrial estates, port facilities and gas, electricity and water supplies. Once again, however, in most Community countries it is difficult to establish the level of investment that has taken place for regional development purposes, and discussion of this issue will therefore be postponed until the EIB's loan strategy is examined later in this chapter.

The Community Dimension to Regional Policy

Given the complexities of national regional policies and the high degree of competition between regions for mobile growth, it was natural that the Commission should at the outset identify policy harmonisation as an appropriate goal for its regional activities (European Parliament, 1960; Lind and Flockton, 1970; McCrone, 1969; Romus, 1975; Armstrong, 1979). The clearest steps that have been taken in this direction relate to the imposition of limits to national aid, whereby governments are required to restrict their assistance to projects in order to ensure that financial support does not exceed a predetermined ceiling. Although proposed in 1966, this system was not accepted by the Council of Ministers until 1971, but since then it has been elaborated to recognise four regional categories, each with its own ceiling expressed in terms of total investment and the ratio between investment and job creation. From Table 4.2 it is apparent that the regional classification and the levels at which ceilings are pitched favour the periphery of the Community, a bias reflecting concern to curb competitive overbidding by the core (Commission of the European Communities, 1976). Although the imposition of aid ceilings may appear to be a progressive attempt to take a broad view of regional problems at the Community level, however, it has not escaped criticism, most forcefully argued by

Table 4.2 *Aid Ceilings Imposed by the European Commission*

| | | Maximum aid | |
		Net grant equivalent as % of initial investment	EUA per job created by initial investment
Ireland	Whole country		
Italy	Mezzogiorno		
West Germany	West Berlin	75 or 13,000	
France	Overseas Depts		
UK	Northern Ireland		
France	Regional Development Premium areas		
Italy	Aided centre-north	30 or 5,500 up to 40%	
UK	Assisted Areas		
West Germany	Zonal Border Area		
Denmark	Special Dev. Regions	25 or 4,500 up to 30%	
Other regions		20 or 3,500 up to 25%	

Source: Commission of the European Communities, 1978.

Yuill, Allen and Hull (1980). Their objections are manifold: the ceilings are not based on detailed analyses of the severity of regional problems; no consideration has been given to the effectiveness of one form of assistance as opposed to another; control may have stifled the emergence of new, more adventurous assistance measures because of the difficulty of gaining acceptance for them; the system is too sweeping in the sense that it applies to all projects rather than being limited to those likely to be mobile at the Community level; and, of considerable importance in a sensitive policy area, terms dictated by the Commission have led to friction and loss of goodwill between Brussels and some national policy-makers.

Yuill, Allen and Hull are clearly of the opinion that these faults arise because the system is the brainchild of the Commission's Competition Directorate (DG IV), which has moved into the regional policy field in its attempts to control what is judged to be unfair assistance by some national governments. In contrast the Regional Policy Directorate (DG XVI), recognising the political minefield which regional policy represents, has adopted an indicative rather than a coercive strategy. Considerable effort has been devoted to identifying and monitoring the most significant interregional disparities within the Community (Commission of the European Communities, 1971, 1980a); recent regional development studies have focused on, for example, the problems of policy evaluation and the mobilisation of the indigenous potential of regions (Commission of the European Communities, 1981a); and steps have been taken to encourage member countries to reexamine their regional policies during the preparation of the Regional Development Programmes submitted to Brussels in the late 1970s. As was indicated in Chapter 1, however, in addition to these attempts to bring about more informed and objective approaches to spatial development problems, various Community agencies are now directly involved in the provision of regional aid. Some of this assistance, provided by the European Social Fund and the European Coal and Steel Community, has been aimed at promoting worker mobility between jobs and, to a lesser extent, between regions (Collins, 1975). But the principal target has been the same as that pursued by national governments – the promotion of industrial development. Finance has been brought to bear on this target

by the ECSC, by the European Investment Bank and by the
European Regional Development Fund.

THE NATURE OF COMMUNITY ASSISTANCE

In contrast to individual member countries, the Community's
regional aid agencies do not offer complex incentive packages.
Instead each agency is heavily reliant on a principal mode of
assistance, with a major distinction as to the nature of this
mode being apparent between the ERDF on the one hand and
the ECSC and the EIB on the other.

ERDF assistance is relatively conventional, being provided
almost entirely in the form of cash grants. For industrial projects these cover 20 per cent of total investment, but with
conditions attached (Talbot, 1978; *Official Journal of the
European Communities*, 1979, C36). For example, following the
principle of 'additionality', projects must qualify for national
subsidisation in order to receive Community support; to
avoid oversubsidisation, aid to private sector developments
cannot exceed 50 per cent of the assistance given by national
authorities; and, to limit the disproportionate consumption of
finite grant resources by capital-hungry schemes, aid may not
exceed 100,000 EUA per job created or 50,000 EUA per job
safeguarded. (At the time of writing, £1 equalled 0·549 units
of account). For infrastructural projects, discrimination is exercised with respect to the scale of the investment programme.
For small infrastructural schemes the grant rate is 30
per cent, for those of more than 10 million EUA it can normally be varied between 10 and 30 per cent, and for projects of
special significance to a region the ceiling may be raised to 40
per cent. Some projects are, of course, rejected as ineligible,
but the failure rate through this cause has been less than 10 per
cent, and a more important statistic is that 11,745 projects
were assisted between 1975 and 1980 (ERDF *Annual Reports*).
Much more significant constraints on the Fund's activities are
imposed by the size of its budget (only a fifth of that enjoyed
by the CAP) and its quota system which, as we shall see,
defines the annual aid to which each country is entitled, irrespective of the projects proposed.

As was seen in Chapter 1, the ECSC and the EIB offer loans
rather than grants, and to this extent their strategies are

unconventional. In general the terms attached to EIB and ECSC loans are similar. Up to 50 per cent of total investment may be advanced, and repayment periods may be negotiated up to twenty years, although in practice a timespan of ten to fifteen years is nearer the norm. Despite this similarity, however, the agencies have contrasted approaches to the question of subsidisation. On this count the ECSC's terms are the more attractive, for in the first five years of a loan a firm may qualify for an interest subsidy of up to 3 per cent, and capital repayments need not take place during an initial four-year 'holiday' period. EIB loans, reflecting the organisation's origins in the Treaty of Rome, have traditionally avoided concessions that could be interpreted as major subsidies to basic investment and operating costs. Only since 1979 has the Bank offered a specific interest subsidy (also a loan 'softening' of up to 3 per cent) and this is funded separately by the Community and is restricted to Ireland and Italy, relatively weak member countries who are full members of the European Monetary System (EIB *Information*, 1979, no. 11).

SPATIAL TARGETS FOR COMMUNITY ASSISTANCE

By definition, ECSC loans cannot be offered on a widespread basis but must instead be focused on problem regions in which the coal and steel industries have been well represented. These regions can also qualify for loans under the EIB's rules, as can all industrial development areas, but the principle that a primary aim of the Bank should be the diminution of major prosperity contrasts throughout the Community has ensured that assistance to low-intensity (peripheral) economies has become a central theme. Activities in this major sphere, coupled with the attention given to declining industrial areas and frontier regions, meant that between 1958 and 1972 the Bank's regional budget accounted for 86 per cent of the value of all loans; and, although in the 1970s there was less proporational emphasis on loans for regional economic improvement, in 1980 two-thirds of the allocations were none the less for projects with a direct regional aid dimension (EIB *Annual Reports*).

In 1977 the European Commission argued that the specific regions qualifying for ERDF aid should be established by the interregional comparison of socioeconomic criteria. These were to include unemployment and migration trends over a five-year period, the size of the agricultural labour force and the proportional importance of declining industries (Commission of the European Communities, 1977a). But these proposals were not adopted by the Council of Ministers, not least because they would have increased the Commission's power to control the spatial allocation of ERDF resources. As in the early years of the Fund's operation, therefore, member countries receive grants according to a quota system (Table 4.3) which the Commission cannot change; and, at least in theory, any region can qualify for aid from this source if it is a national development area.

Although the Commission, working through its Regional Policy Directorate, is therefore subject to considerable restrictions, in three respects it has been given at least some influence over the geographical targeting of finance. When the ERDF was established the Regulation defining its operations stipulated that preference should be given to projects in regions designated as priority areas by national regional policies (*Official Journal of the European Communities*, 1975, L73). This has been underlined by the Regional Policy Directorate, governments have responded by submitting project proposals mainly selected from these areas, and there has therefore been substantial adherence to the guideline. For example, in 1980 (the most recent year for which details are available) 86 per cent of ERDF aid to West Germany was channelled into priority areas; in France and the UK the proportions were 86 per cent and 78 per cent respectively; and all aid to Italy and the Netherlands went to districts in this category.

Secondly, the Commission's influence has increased because, after prolonged resistance, in 1978 the Council of Ministers accepted that there should be a non-quota section for the ERDF (ERDF, *Annual Report*, 1978). Control of this finance lies with the Commission's ERDF Committee, which may support 'multiannual development programmes' to ameliorate regional problems arising from a frontier location, from the impact of global trends in major industries, or from the application of non-regional Community policies. So far, assistance under this heading has been given to Ireland and Northern Ireland for frontier problems; to the UK, Italy and

Table 4.3 National Allocation of ECSC, EIB and ERDF Regional Assistance, 1978–80 (%)

	ECSC worker retraining grants (1980)	ECSC regional restructuring loans (1978–80 av.)	EIB regional development loans (1978–80 av.)	NCI regional loans (1979–80 av.)	ERDF quotas (1980)	ERDF quotas (1981)
Belgium	0·8	1·9	0·3	—	1·39	1·11
Denmark	—	—	2·0	—	1·20	1·06
West Germany	3·7	13·8	0·1	—	6·00	4·65
France	6·7	18·6	10·6	—	16·86	13·64
Ireland	0·5	0·7	14·1	43·1	6·46	5·94
Italy	—	2·0	45·4	48·2	39·39	35·49
Luxembourg	4·3	2·3	—	—	0·09	0·07
Netherlands	—	1·1	—	—	1·58	1·24
United Kingdom	84·0	59·6	27·5	8·7	27·03	23·80
Greece	—	—	—	—	—	13·00
	100·0	100·0	100·0	100·0	100·00	100·00
Total allocations (averages for years shown in million EUA)	67·0	220·5	1,614·6	148·9	1,165·0	

Sources: Commission of the European Communities, 1981a; EIB Information, 1981, no. 24; EIB Annual Report, 1978, 1979.

Belgium for industries, especially steel, affected by world trends; and to the Mezzogiorno and southern French regions in connection with the policy of Community enlargement in the Mediterranean. Although the Commission welcomed the introduction of non-quota finance as a significant progressive step, however, the fact that it was restricted to a mere 5 per cent of the total ERDF budget caused continuing dissatisfaction and pressure for change (see Chapter 5).

Thirdly, against the background of deepening recession, in 1978 the Council of Ministers approved the Commission's proposal for a New Community Instrument (NCI), a financial measure designed to increase support for infrastructural and energy projects, especially those with a major regional dimension (Commission of the European Communities, 1981a; EIB *Information*, 1979, no. 19). Because this measure is essentially a borrowing and lending arrangement its administration and the final selection of projects are channelled through the EIB rather than the ERDF. Yet decision-making on the eligibility of applications is vested with the Commission, and in 1979/80 these loans were focused on the UK (8·7 per cent), Ireland (43·1 per cent) and Italy (48·2 per cent). As with non-quota ERDF finance, however, NCI resources have been restricted in scale: in this two-year period they were equivalent to only 3·6 per cent of the EIB's regionally oriented loans, although they did increase by a fifth the finance available to Ireland through the EIB.

While it is important to establish the background to the spatial policies of Community agencies, it is also relevant to investigate the extent to which these policies have recently overlapped to reinforce both each other and national strategies. Table 4.3 allows comparisons to be made between countries, but it must be emphasised that, because the data are presented as percentages, contrasts of scale between the agencies are disguised. ECSC conversion loans normally amount to 200–300 million EUA a year, compared with the EIB's 1980 allocation of 1,815·7 million EUA for regional development projects and with the ERDF's 1980 budget of 1,165 million EUA.

It is apparent that the overlap between the agencies' spatial targets is not perfect. The EIB, for example, directed only 10 per cent of its regionally oriented loans into the French economy in the late 1970s, and virtually nothing into West Germany, whereas both these countries were targets for the ECSC because of the presence of the coal and steel industries. Similarly the ERDF has recently allocated a larger proportion of its resources to France and West Germany than has the EIB, this being the outcome of the political negotiations which established the quotas awarded to member countries; and, conversely, the quota system has dictated that the ERDF gives much less emphasis to Ireland than does the EIB.

Apart from these distinctions, much common ground can be identified. In addition to the EIB's avoidance of West Germany, and to a lesser extent France, all three agencies treat Belgium, the Netherlands, Luxembourg and Denmark as minor recipients of aid; Italy is the prime target for both the EIB and the ERDF; and (with the exception of the ECSC's largely unavoidable neglect of Ireland) the UK and Ireland have been treated as a major aid-absorbing bloc that has arisen in the Community since its 1973 expansion. Thus, although the agencies interpret regional economic problems as being essentially structural in nature, it is apparent that this interpretation has a powerful spatial dimension strongly reminiscent of the centre–periphery model. Aid to central problem regions is clearly a subsidiary theme, with the large majority of the finance being channelled into two foci at the north-western and southern-eastern extremities of the Community (EIB and ERDF *Annual Reports*; EIB, 1978; EIB *Information*, 1977, no. 11, 1979, no. 19). This high degree of aid concentration is, of course, underlined if these foci are considered in more detail for, in the main, northern Italy has been allocated to the 'centre' category, as have South East England and the Midlands.

Finally in this section, it can be anticipated that further changes in spatial targeting will occur as the second expansion phase progresses. The UK-Ireland focus will certainly remain and, on paper at least, will be bolstered temporarily by the special regional aid (in 1981, 955 million EUA) negotiated to reduce Britain's net contribution to Community funds. But the south-eastern focus should strengthen as finance to Greece increases (EIB *Information*, 1981, no. 21), and it should then broaden as Spain and Portugal join the competition for Community assistance. Quite possibly this will necessitate rapid

expansion of the EIB's loan activities, and a proposal to reallo-
cate ERDF quota funds is in part a response to this emerging
problem (see Table 5.1 page 110).

SECTORAL TARGETS FOR REGIONAL DEVELOPMENT

Current ERDF and EIB regulations make it possible for
service sector schemes (such as tourism) and agricultural
improvement programmes to qualify for assistance but, as has
already been indicated, the Community's loans and grants are
overwhelmingly aimed at manufacturing and public sector
infrastructural developments. In the case of the ECSC the
allocation of aid between these two principal targets has been
firmly in favour of manufacturing, although some infrastructural loans have gone to support the construction of industrial
estates and the provision of housing for displaced workers.
Both the EIB and the ERDF, on the other hand, have channelled the major part of their finance into infrastructure under
the EOC heading, following the principle that this is an essential prerequisite for healthy manufacturing expansion in the
assisted areas. Thus between 1958 and the mid-1970s two-
thirds of the EIB's loans were for infrastructural projects,
while the ERDF devoted an almost identical proportion of its
grants to infrastructure in 1978–80. ERDF funding in this
field is too recent to establish significant trends, but from
observation of the EIB's experience of loan administration,
which now extends over more than two decades, it is immediately apparent that commitment to EOC funding has not
meant inflexible adherence to initial investment targets (Table
4.4).

One major change has been a rapid expansion of energy
investments: until the early 1970s energy projects accounted
for a quarter of all the Bank's infrastructural loans, but in the
period 1972–80 the corresponding proportion was a half. This
rapid development reflected, of course, the Commission's
desire to strengthen and diversify the Community's energy
base in the aftermath of the 1973 oil crisis, and for this reason
most of the energy loans made in the 1970s were not made
specifically for regional development. It is possible to interpret
this as a weakening of the Bank's regional orientation, yet a
regional dimension to the change can none the less be iden-

Table 4.4   *European Investment Bank Infrastructural Loans, 1958–80*

	1958–71 (%)	1972–80 (%)
Energy	24·7	48·5
of which: *nuclear power*	*2·6*	*19·0*
other electricity generation	*15·6*	*10·5*
development of oil and gas deposits	*0·0*	*5·1*
gas and oil pipelines	*6·5*	*8·0*
other energy	*0·0*	*5·9*
Conventional communications	46·2	13·2
of which: *roads*	*32·2*	*6·7*
Telecommunications	16·5	18·5
Water supply and distribution	2·5	19·2
Other	10·1	0·6
	100·0	100·0
Total infrastructural loans (million EUA):	1,094·4	9,636·2

Sources: EIB *Annual Reports*; EIB *Information*, 1981, no. 24; Pinder, 1978.

tified, for industrialisation policies are likely to be impeded by energy problems inhibiting security and prosperity at the national level (EIB, 1978, EIB *Information*, 1980, no. 23).

Trends in non-energy infrastructural investment have been equally dynamic. In its early years the EIB invested heavily in a variety of 'conventional' communications projects, including railways, waterways, ports and airports, but with the improvement of the Community's motorway network as the prime target. Motorways absorbed more than half the conventional communications investments before 1972, a degree of emphasis which, from a regional policy viewpoint, owed much to the argument that improved interregional contact would intensify economic activity and ameliorate centre–periphery contrasts by accelerating the trickling-down process (Pinder, 1978). Between 1972 and 1980, however, conventional communications accounted for only an eighth of the Bank's infrastructural investments, compared with almost half before 1972. Although this relative decline partly reflects the fact that the Community's major road network is now much nearer completion than in the 1960s, it is also symptomatic of the growing view that transportation improvements do not guarantee more equable centre–periphery balance. Polarisation, rather than trickling down, may be accentuated by the reduction of regional isolation, especially if other aspects of regional EOC investment remain unsatisfactory, and it is therefore significant that the Bank has focused increasingly on less well-known infrastructural targets: telecommunications, water supplies and sewerage schemes (EIB, 1978; EIB *Information*, 1977, no. 10, 1980, no. 21). Physically different though they are, the economic rationale behind these new emphases is that if these services are deficient in volume and reliability this will impede both the attraction of firms to lagging regions and the realisation of growth potential among indigenous businesses.

In the 1970s telecommunications and water-management projects accounted for almost 40 per cent of all infrastructural investments, with the allocations being geographically widespread in the periphery: an arc of telecommunications improvement has extended from southern Italy through western France to Ireland, while water and sewerage schemes have been located as far apart as Apulia and northern Britain. In Apulia, and elsewhere in southern Italy, water schemes have benefited both agriculture and industry, the sewerage projects being primarily intended for urban and industrial nodes such as Naples. Water and sewerage schemes have been widespread in Ireland, and recent loans to Britain have been dominated by projects (including the Kielder Reservoir in Northumbria) to improve services for the conurbations of northern England and Scotland.

So far as industrial loans and grants are concerned, all three Community agencies spread their assistance over a wide range of activities, much in the manner of national governments. Despite the breadth of the investment front, however, certain preferences connected with growth-pole theory can be identified. Coal and steel, two traditional growth-pole industries, have of course benefited from the ECSC's position of special responsibility for their long-term future: loans to rebuild these basic industries have recently been two or three times as much as those to new industries involved in regional restructuring programmes. Similarly the steel industry has been a prominent recipient of EIB funds, as in the context of transplanting the industry to Taranto in southern Italy; and in the first thirteen years of the Bank's operations no less than a third of its industrial loans were devoted to the rapid expansion of the chemicals industry. Here the accent has been on petrochemicals and the development of a wide product range providing essential inputs for many other industries, with southern Italy, plus the Italian islands, again being a major beneficiary of the policy.

The importance attached to the cultivation of growth-pole activities has not, however, been overwhelming. The electrical engineering and electronics industries have absorbed less than 6 per cent of the industrial loans made since the EIB's foundation in 1958 and, although the motor vehicle and transport-equipment industries attracted a fifth of the industrial loans made in the period 1977–80, previously their share was less than 10 per cent. It is also notable that the EIB's rates of investment in the basic metal and chemicals industries have fallen recently, the decline being particularly abrupt in the case of chemicals. Several factors, of which recession is only the most obvious, have contributed to the shift away from these investment targets. Because of the nature of their capital equipment, industries such as steel and chemicals are expensive to develop and investment costs per job are therefore high – often as much as £100,000. Moreover, cost and safety considerations normally dictate that employment is minimised, so that a project's manpower demands soon reach a plateau and do not offer steadily increasing job opportunities in the host region. Although emphasis may be placed on sustaining employment expansion by attracting linked industries to the key investment, the results are often disappointing, mainly because of the liberating influence of improved communications and technology noted in Chapter 3. When linked activities are not attracted, centres reliant on implanted growth-pole industries possess narrowly based economies that afford little employment choice and, eventually, are highly likely to become outmoded.

Realisation of these drawbacks has not been confined to the EIB or to other Community agencies; but the Bank has been particularly responsive to them, one major outcome being the introduction of a new industrialisation strategy, the global loan system, in 1968. Global loans are made by the EIB to banks and other financial institutions, which in turn act as intermediaries disbursing the loans, with the Bank's approval, to numerous small- and medium-scale industrial concerns in problem regions. Within the Bank's overall operations this system has proved popular: in 1981, 65 per cent of its industrial loan finance was allocated in this way. Moreover, the concept has been adopted by the ECSC and modified by the ERDF to apply to its grant scheme; and it has been broadened, admittedly on a modest scale, to apply to infrastructural projects as well as to manufacturing (EIB *Information*, 1980, no. 21, 1981, no. 24).

The advantages claimed for allocating global loans to problem regions are, of course, largely the mirror image of the disadvantages associated with growth-pole implantations. Job creation is cheap, usually only a fifth of that needed in major industrial schemes. Total employment in a group of firms may equal or exceed the manpower of a single 'showpiece' project, and there is the possibility that this total could continue to increase with the allocation of further global loans. Manufacturing variety offers the benefit of employment choice, while it also reduces long-term obsolescence problems: some firms may fail, yet it is improbable that all would experience concurrent economic crises. Also, instead of aiming at self-sufficiency, small and medium-sized firms may stimulate local industry and services, thereby producing more vigorous multiplier effects. In addition, the process of expanding manufacturing need rely less heavily on overcoming perception barriers in order to divert growth from successful regions to development areas. Global loans and grants are well suited to the needs of firms indigenous to problem regions and they therefore seek to exploit the potential internal growth in the 'nursery' of a regional economy.

From this survey it is apparent that a major assault on regional economic problems has been mounted in the postwar period. Most Community countries have tackled these problems in a similar manner and, although governments have naturally given prominence to the internal problems of their regional systems, significant competition for internationally mobile growth has also arisen. This trend was virtually dictated by the political map of Western Europe, and it has worked to the advantage of the core. Much of the European Community's effort has been intended to tip the balance in favour of the periphery, a basic policy theme identifiable despite the weaknesses of the ERDF and despite the fragmentation of Community assistance between different agencies. Given this intensive national and international effort, one major question is unavoidable: to what extent have regional policies borne fruit? This question provides the starting point for Chapter 5.

5 *Retrospect and Prospect*

Recent emphasis on the evaluation of regional policy stems partly from the belief that at least limited progress can be anticipated over a relatively short timespan, but also from accusations that taxpayers' money has been squandered on ineffective measures. At the most fundamental level the issue is clear: is it legitimate to claim that 'it would be better for [countries] to concentrate resources at those points where they would yield earlier returns and . . . also a more viable return' (House of Commons Expenditure Committee, 1972, p. 218)? At the Community level Marquand (1980a) has argued that the pursuit of non-spatial Community policies has tended to exacerbate regional problems, but the extent to which spatial policy has acted as a countervailing force has yet to be investigated deeply. The discussion must therefore focus on the conclusions to be drawn from national programmes although, on the basis of these conclusions, it is possible to consider the future of regional policies in a Community facing great economic uncertainty as the twentieth century draws to a close.

Evaluation Problems

Three difficulties relating to the problem of evaluation must be noted at the outset. The first is the paradox that, although the intention to undertake evaluation implies the existence of goals which may be used as yardsticks, in practice goals may be poorly defined and are highly likely to vary as governments and economic circumstances change. Laxity in goal definition has been heavily attacked by Emanuel (1973). Very different conclusions may emerge if the assumed goal is taken to be the acceleration of employment creation rather than the generation of sufficient employment to compensate for industrial decline or to achieve a significant reduction in interregional prosperity contrasts.

Secondly, regional policy has not been the only force affecting the 'trajectory' of regions in economic space. Since the early postwar years a major rearrangement has taken place in the relative importance of economic sectors as agriculture has contracted to achieve greater efficiency and industry and services have grown. The geography of these sectoral shifts has been well documented (Commission of the European Communities, 1971), while Molle, Van Holst and Smit (1980) have shown that the consequence of sectoral evolution was convergence towards more uniform regional economic structures. Broad evidence of reduced interregional disparity was associated with this convergence, especially with respect to GDP per capita and per employee; it was also indicated by the shares of Community GDP generated by selected proportions of the population. These trends were in line with Community goals, but the fact that they became firmly established in the 1950s, before the intensive application of regional policy, demonstrates the importance of non-spatial policies and autonomous forces in regional economic evolution. A major problem afflicting the evaluation process is, therefore, the identification of changes which can be attributed with certainty to the implementation of regional policy.

The third difficulty is that the methods employed in the search for this certainty have been the subject of considerable controversy. *Shift-share techniques*, which compare a region's industrial performance with that of the nation as a whole over a given time period, have been favoured by many investigators, but they are associated with a variety of conceptual and technical pitfalls. Among other things, the results are sensitive to the degree of generalisation in the input data and to the scale of the regions investigated. Moreover, while the shift-share approach and its variants describe the ways in which actual regional performance deviates from expectation, no explanatory variables are built into the calculations. It is therefore difficult to be certain that deviations from expectation are the consequence of regional policy rather than of other factors (Vanhove and Klaassen, 1980). *Linear modelling* attempts to overcome this drawback by employing multiple regression techniques to replicate regional performance statistically. When successful the resulting model should not only explain a very high proportion of regional growth observable in a given period, it should also allow conclusions to be drawn with respect to the relative importance of explanatory variables such as the types of incentives employed. But regression techniques must also be treated cautiously. Richardson (1978b) has expressed reservations relating chiefly to the inadequacy of input data and the models' neglect of space, while Schofield (1979) has underlined the need to ensure that input data fulfil the complex statistical assumptions of multiple regression techniques.

Imperfect though they may be, shift-share analysis and linear modelling have been the chief tools employed in policy evaluation, and attention must therefore be given to the results arising from their use. Because more evaluation exercises have been conducted in Britain than elsewhere in the Community, it is appropriate that this work should be considered first.

Progress in Britain, *c*. 1950–70

A common thread can be identified in much of the literature, for many investigators have sought to exploit the fact that regional policy was not pursued firmly throughout most of the 1950s. This decade is therefore seen as a 'policy-weak' or 'policy-off' period, a datum decade which may be compared with the 1960s, when policy was applied much more rigorously. Most studies do not extend far into the 1970s, however, and the evaluations therefore focus on the heyday of regional policy, before the onset of severe recession. The investigations, well documented by Schofield (1979) and discussed by Hare (1977), have been pursued at a variety of scales (sub-regional, regional and national) and have considered a range of criteria. While recognising this diversity, this discussion will focus on the development areas as a whole and on progress towards employment creation, since this has been a fundamental policy goal. It should be noted that a number of employment estimates have been converted into annual averages to facilitate comparison between studies covering slightly different timespans, but this does not imply that gains were uniform throughout the study periods.

Department of Employment figures quoted by Schofield (1976) suggest that projects planned to create 360,000 jobs were launched in the development areas between 1961 and 1966. If this estimate is scaled down by a quarter, or even by a half, to allow for the notorious tendency of projects to fall below expectation, this official growth estimate remains substantial – somewhere between 26,000 and 33,000 new jobs per year. This range is compatible with Brown's (1972) results and with the most optimistic estimate produced by Moore and Rhodes in a series of controversial studies (Moore and Rhodes, 1975). Their principal finding was that the minimum number of jobs attributable to regional policy in the period 1963–70 was 260,000. This figure was then raised to between 275,000 and 350,000 by adding multiplier effects and by varying assumptions relating to interregional population movements. These estimates give average annual job-creation rates of 32,000 and 44,000 but, before such optimistic conclusions are accepted too readily, account must be taken of work such as that by Buck and Atkins (1976), Mackay (1976) and Massey (1979). While agreeing with Moore and Rhodes that policy became much more effective after 1963, Mackay has concluded that policy-induced employment growth in the four main development areas averaged no more than 21,000 jobs in the post-1963 era. Similarly, the results offered by Buck and Atkins indicate that policy-induced growth averaged only 11,000 jobs per year between 1963 and 1971 and, although this figure is for male employment only and does not include Northern Ireland, the authors stress that in their opinion the estimate is very generous. Massey, meanwhile, has not denied the existence of a direct policy effect, but has argued that an unknown proportion of the estimated employment growth was attributable to industries' search for low-skill labour suitable for automated production methods associated with new forms of business organisation. Thus, while there is general agreement that regional policy was instrumental in achieving employment creation in Britain's development areas in the 1960s, there is no unanimity as to the scale of the impact.

Two further issues relating to British experience must be considered. The first is the question of the relative importance of the forces that have influenced industrial decision-makers to expand in development areas. As Richardson (1978b) and Schofield (1976, 1979) have noted, investigations of this problem have been incomplete in the sense that the possible effects of infrastructure investment have been virtually ignored. This is a potentially fruitful research field, but for the present it must be accepted that conclusions to date are based on analyses of market forces and direct policy instruments. The consensus view is that the principal market force, pressure of demand causing industry to turn voluntarily to development areas for labour, has exerted very little effect. For example, Moore and Rhodes (1976a, 1976b) have estimated by means of regression analysis that no more than 12 per cent of all industrial movement to the development areas in the 1960s can be attributed to labour availability, and Ashcroft and Taylor (1979) have confirmed the weakness of this factor. In contrast, the control exerted by the IDC system and the attractive effects of incentives are acknowledged to have been appreciable interrelated policy instruments, despite the cautious attitude recently adopted by the Department of Industry (1981). In the late 1960s tightening of the IDC system made it much more effective in decentralising investment from the South-East (Sant, 1975) and, after strengthening legislation in 1963, incentives became sufficiently attractive to enable the development areas to capitalise on increased dispersal from the leader region. However, various estimates of the relative importance of controls and incentives have been offered.

From their regression analysis of industrial movement Moore and Rhodes (1976a and 1976b, reported in Keeble, 1976) calculated that, on average, IDC controls were responsible for forty-five relocations to the development areas each year, as opposed to thirty-six relocations attributable to investment grants. From this it was estimated that incentives accounted for 40 or 50 per cent of employment growth arising from movement. Ashcroft and Taylor attributed two-thirds of the development areas' gains to incentives and, in common with Moore and Rhodes, they identified investment incentives available after 1963 as the most powerful weapon in the armoury. Allowing for different periods of operation, the effect of these incentives was at least twice as great as that of Special Development Area assistance, but there is less agreement about the impact of the Regional Employment Premium, the labour subsidy introduced in 1967 to counterbalance capital grants. Moore and Rhodes concluded that the power of labour subsidies was intermediate between the effects of normal capital grants and Special Development Area assistance; Mackay (1976) detected less sign of a positive effect in the late 1960s, while Buck and Atkins (1976) associated labour subsidies with a period of reduced policy effectiveness.

Secondly it is pertinent to consider whether the ill-defined improvements catalogued above represent a net gain or loss for the country as a whole. The literature, reviewed by Schofield (1976), is less profuse with respect to this issue, but Schofield's paper presents an analysis which both confirms and qualifies the cost-benefit work of Moore and Rhodes (1975).

Moore and Rhodes's thesis is that, from a national viewpoint, regional policy in the 1960s was clearly beneficial. Although the exchequer lost resources as a result of direct policy expenditure, it recorded a net gain on tax and social security receipts because of higher aggregate employment; also other net gains accrued from, for example, employment associated with infrastructure and public service expenditure. All in all, gross exchequer costs were three times as great as net costs and, although these net costs were equivalent to a budget deficit of almost £100 million a year, it is argued that net savings not counted in the analysis financed the deficits and made the budgetary implications minimal. Schofield's estimates, based on a range of assumptions, show in all cases a surplus of benefits over costs, thereby supporting Moore and Rhodes's contention that regional policy has not been a drain on the economy. What is also noteworthy, however, is the range of his estimates of net benefit: between £54 million and £958 million over three-year periods. For a variety of reasons discussed in the paper these estimates may be generous, and it is therefore clear that, even if it is accepted that regional policy has been profitable, it is virtually impossible to establish the degree to which this is true. Furthermore, although Schofield does not discuss the point, an interesting distinction between the periods 1960–3 and 1964–6 emerges from his analyses.

Cost-benefit ratios were most favourable in the earlier period, and it therefore appears that the intensification of regional policy after 1963 was associated with diminishing returns per unit of cost.

In summary, therefore, British experience indicates that decentralisation from leader regions can be achieved, that incentive systems are necessary to divert at least a proportion of the movement to development areas, that the growth rate of development area employment can be raised, and that the costs of achieving this progress need not outweigh the benefits for a national economy. Beyond this, however, it is evident that much remains unsolved. This is particularly true with respect to the scale of employment creation, a point which must be related to the fact that the goals against which investigators have measured the success of regional policy have been relatively restricted. In most instances the aim has been to establish whether development area performance, primarily as measured by job creation and industrial movement, was significantly better in the 1960s than in the 1950s, and the general conclusion that this was the case has been taken to indicate policy success. Cost-benefit analysis has recognised that the evaluation problem can be approached from other directions, yet most of these have not been examined in depth. The extent to which policy-induced growth has been able to compensate for the contraction of specific problem industries is a case in point, while trends in per capita incomes, per capita GDP and unemployment are further examples. It is true that some studies have considered evaluating other criteria and have rejected them on the grounds of unreliability; yet the fact remains that most regional policies were initiated in anticipation that, as well as raising employment growth in lagging regions, intervention would contribute to the permanent reduction of interregional socioeconomic disparities. Moreover, at the Community level it has long been argued that severe interregional prosperity contrasts are serious obstacles to unity and stability. As we move on to consider other parts of the Community, therefore, it is necessary to ask whether genuine progress towards broader regional policy goals has been achieved.

Experience in Other Community Countries

This section considers trends in three other Community countries (France, the Netherlands, and Ireland), in one prospective member (Spain) and in two major problem regions drawn from the Community's core and periphery (southern Belgium and southern Italy). Because these areas are strongly differentiated with respect to size, location, economic structure and the nature and intensity of regional problems, they provide a diverse picture for comparison with British experience.

FRANCE

Prud'homme (1974), House (1978), Tuppen (1980) and Clout (1981) have provided useful evaluations of French policy between the 1950s and the mid-1970s. So far as timing is concerned, certain similarities with Britain can be observed. Control in the Paris region and incentives in limited development areas came in the mid-1950s, but incentives were initially very weak, and the 1960s and early 1970s therefore witnessed a series of strengthening measures, together with the expansion of designated development areas. As with the IDC system, control measures have undoubtedly been effective in inducing the decentralisation of economic activity from Paris, but the main successes were achieved in the early 1960s, after which the annual decentralisation rate declined from more than 250 establishments to less than 50 in the mid-1970s. Another similarity with Britain is that policy-induced mobility has not automatically benefited development areas; at least 50 per cent of the decentralising firms have opted for locations outside the assisted regions, especially in centres approximately 150–200 km from the capital. This strong preference for short-distance decentralisation appears at least partly attributable to weaknesses in the incentive system: during the 1960s expenditure was not escalated on a scale equivalent to that in Britain. Although House emphasises the extent of structural change in individual regions, Tuppen and Clout are agreed that, broadly speaking, the volume of industrialisation attributable to policy in the development areas as a whole has been a clear disappointment. Similarly Prud'homme has concluded that there is little to suggest that regional policy exerted a beneficial effect on income disparities in the 1960s, although it must be acknowledged that progress on this count may have been disguised by reductions in the rate of out-migration from economically weak regions. Despite this qualification, it does not appear that the influence exerted by the renowned school of French regional economists and planners was matched with great success.

THE NETHERLANDS

The principal statistical investigation of Dutch policy relates to the period 1960–7, which followed a significant expansion and intensification of regional policy in 1959 (although an important point of contrast with Britain and France was that the changes did not include the introduction of leader-region control). Regression was again the basic investigative tool, the most relevant result being that 35 per cent of development area employment growth could be considered to be policy-induced (Vanhove and Klaassen, 1980). However, this finding must be qualified. It is true that by the early 1970s the most extensive problem region (the North) showed several signs of progress. Dependence on special employment projects was greatly reduced, endemic out-migration was virtually eliminated, and the region's share of national industrial employment corresponded closely with its share of population. Yet growth industries' share of regional employment remained below the national average, despite the fact that the Philips electronics firm had become the largest regional employer, and a bias towards low-wage industries could be detected. Also, from the mid-1960s onwards, development centres experienced increasing difficulties in attracting new employers, seasonal unemployment remained more pronounced than in any other part of the country and seasonally corrected unemployment levels stayed stubbornly above the national figure (Pinder, 1976).

IRELAND

The most thorough investigation of Ireland's regional policy has been undertaken by O'Farrell (1978). A substantial part of O'Farrell's study is concerned with the analysis of new firms' propensity to locate inside and outside the development areas, statistical tests being applied to identify associations between location and the characteristics of firms. A striking feature of the results is that location does not appear to have been strongly influenced by the size of new projects, by their sectoral origin, by their markets, or by their degree of capital-intensity. Similarly, neither indigenous growth nor multinational capital, the volume of which has been highly impressive, can be shown to have been biased in favour of, or against, the development areas. Yet O'Farrell did identify one significant association, namely, between the application of capital grant incentives and the flow of firms to development areas. Unfortunately, the volume of growth attributable to this association was not quantified, but there is none the less evidence of incentive impact, and it is argued that the strength of the association merits more widespread use of heavy investment subsidies.

SPAIN

Lasuén's (1974) study of the Spanish regional system covers a longer timespan than those of other commentators and considers the spatial impact of several policies other than the main industrialisation initiatives. His interpretation of pre-Civil War circumstances is that impressive infrastructural policies were pursued, affecting the road and rail networks and water supplies, but that this did little except demonstrate that it can be extremely difficult to weaken polarisation forces unless infrastructure programmes are complemented by substantial decentralisation measures. Postwar economic policy favoured maximum national growth, savings on infrastructural expenditure (facilitated by earlier investments) and autarchic national development. Although lip-service was paid to the spatial impact of these policies, scant action was taken to accelerate regional economic development, and the country therefore experienced a lengthy 'policy-off' phase during which regional divergence became more firmly entrenched. Regional income data indicate that this trend ended in the 1960s, but the improvement appears to have been reinforced rather than initiated by regional policy. Much more important were the natural dynamics of the economy and, in particular, the rise of multiproduct firms well suited to branch-plant development in areas of labour availability. Moreover, except in the Basque country and in Catalonia, urban centres did not exert far-reaching stimuli in surrounding rural areas, and interregional convergence was therefore accompanied by divergent rural–urban income differentials. The effect of this was to widen the gulf between urban and rural societies in the national periphery.

It is apparent that these national surveys largely confirm British experience, both with respect to progress and to limitations. Inattention to regional policies in Spain contributed to intensified spatial disequilibria, the recent amelioration of which is attributable only in uncertain measure to the application of regional policy; control measures in the Paris region enjoyed early success which has dwindled without being fully exploited for the benefit of development areas; and the experiences of France, the Netherlands and Ireland reveal a positive, yet ill-defined, relationship between incentive strength and growth prospects. Only qualified success can be claimed and, as the final examples demonstrate, in some major regions the uncertainty surrounding progress towards stated policy goals is very considerable.

SOUTHERN BELGIUM

This major francophone region, which occupies Belgium south of Brussels, is an economically diverse zone that has experienced sharp contraction of rural and industrial activities, the details of change being well documented by the Commission of the European Communities (1979c) and Vanhove and Klaassen (1980). Regional policy, discussed by Thoman (1973) and Riley (1976), was first applied in 1959, with the immediate aim of compensating for employment losses experienced in the 1950s and anticipated in the 1960s. Throughout the 'policy-on' period incentives have, of course, been available in designated areas, but in restricted districts ordinary assistance was supplemented in 1966 by the introduction of 'exceptional' aid. Policy was also reinforced in the mid-1960s by the expansion of infrastructural investment, most particularly through the construction of a motorway network. By providing excellent intraregional, interregional and international connections, this road-building programme has enabled southern Belgium to offer industrialists locations with almost unrivalled access to major Community markets. In addition, to increase the region's attractions still further, more than fifty industrial estates offer incentives and many are linked with the motorway system.

Thoman has stressed that, although the growth potential of some incentive-assisted firms was weak, southern Belgium attracted investment totalling almost 200 billion Belgian francs between 1959 and 1970. Moreover, following the 1966 policy revision and the initiation of large-scale infrastructural investment, the coalfield provinces attracted 40 per cent of foreign investment entering Belgium in the late 1960s. Despite these encouraging indicators, however, only limited progress was made towards the goal of compensation for employment decline. Official statistics for the period 1960–74 (i.e. from the initiation of regional policy to the onset of world recession) show that 74,000 coalmining jobs were lost, as were 21,000 in the steel industry. Yet the industrial estates, the prime locations intended to attract incoming growth, generated no more than 38,000 jobs, only 29,000 of which were definitely new opportunities rather than employment transfers. Thus the balance sheet probably recorded an employment deficit of between 57,000 and 66,000, figures that would appear substantially worse if the study period was lengthened to include the 'policy-off' years of the 1950s. Vanhove and Klaassen have, in fact, taken a longer time perspective, their estimates for 1950–70 being a net loss of 165,000 in mining and manufacturing and of 135,000 across all sectors. In contrast northern Belgium, excluding Brussels, increased industrial employment by 50,000 and total employment by 166,000 in these years.

SOUTHERN ITALY (THE MEZZOGIORNO)

A truly severe North/South development gap in the Italian economy was already apparent in the late nineteenth century, when weak industrial development began to leave a poor and large population heavily dependent on a backward agricultural sector. Emigration became an escape mechanism and, although economic dualism became a major political issue in the early 1900s, at mid-century the centre–periphery mould remained unbroken. In 1950 only 27 per cent of southern employment was provided by industry, compared with an average of 44 per cent in central and northern regions; 39 per cent of employment was still based on agriculture, almost twice the proportion found elsewhere; and structural weakness in agriculture and industry ensured that earnings, and therefore regional demand, remained depressed. In the early 1950s average per capita income was little more than half that enjoyed by the North, a disparity which exerted an obvious undermining influence on the strength of multiplier effects (Chenery, 1962; Barzanti, 1965).

Four characteristics of the Mezzogiorno's policy-on period, which dates from approximately 1950, must be noted. First, several distinct phases can be identified within the broad period. Until 1957 agricultural reform and redressing the shortfall in public facilities held sway; thereafter industrialisation became a major policy plank (Nocifora, 1978); from 1965 onwards greater attention was given to project co-ordination; and in the 1970s a measure of decision-making power was devolved within the region as a reaction against strong centralisation (EIB *Information*, 1977, no. 11). Secondly, industrialisation policy has been linked with the country's extensive nationalisation programme in an attempt to accelerate the transplantation of employment from North to South. Thirdly, despite the turbulence of Italian politics an element of stability in policy implementation has been provided by the main intervention agency, the *Cassa per il Mezzogiorno* (Fund for the South). And, fourthly, emphasis on industrialisation has been strongly supported by international aid, the most outstanding examples being EIB loans and, more recently, ERDF grants. Thus regional development efforts have evolved, have been strengthened and have been diversified in a variety of ways. One third of the capital investment between 1951 and 1974 was linked in some way with assistance (EIB *Information*, 1977, no. 11), and it is against this background of intensive long-term intervention in the Nine's most outstanding problem region that progress towards closing North/South differentials must be judged.

The EIB (*Information*, 1977, no. 11, 1979, no. 19) and Graziani (1978) have emphasised the far-reaching changes experienced by the Mezzogiorno up to the oil crisis of 1973. Agriculture shed more than 2 million workers and industrial employment rose from 27 to 35 per cent of the labour force. Whereas in 1951 the region accounted for only 15 per cent of Italian industrial investment, the corresponding proportion in 1973 was 44 per cent. Industrial productivity, measured as a proportion of the national average, had risen from 64 to 71 per cent; and in many places educational facilities, transport, water supplies and sanitation had improved dramatically with the implementation of infrastructural programmes. However, examination of a wide range of socioeconomic criteria in the 1950–70 period has demonstrated that progress was not sufficient to narrow substantially the North/South development gap (Cao-Pinna, 1974). For example, by the early 1970s the Mezzogiorno's contribution to Italian industrial GDP was still less than 20 per cent; between 1960 and 1970 the region's share of national unemployment rose from 38 to 45 per cent; and, in constant prices, southern per capita income in 1971 was only equivalent to that of north-west Italy in 1951.

Several theories to account for this inability of absolute progress to erode relative backwardness have been discussed by Graziani, who has attributed much of the difficulty to the emergence of a vicious circle in the development process. According to this thesis, impressive investment in basic industry in the Mezzogiorno has created new demand for consumer and producer goods. To a great extent, however, this larger market has been satisfied by producers outside the region, and their competitive edge has led to the decline of local industries which formerly served internal markets. In a sense, therefore, the effect of the development programme has been to damage the cumulative causation mechanism rather than strengthen it. The consequence of this has been that continued subsidisation by other regions has become necessary to fuel the southern economy. This has completed the vicious circle and has ensured that, although the Mezzogiorno is much less poor than was previously the case, earlier self-sufficiency levels have been undermined and replaced by a high degree of dependence on more prosperous Italian regions.

Non-Spatial Policies and Development Inequalities

In retrospect it is apparent that, although economic growth has been cultivated in many economically weak regions, achievements have often failed to equate with short-term expectations. As the OECD observed (1974, p. 138), 'We cannot point to any country that has been able . . . to achieve the objectives it has set for itself'; and it may be that Hall's (1974) conclusion that regional policy has enabled British development areas to run in order to stand still is also widely applicable to the Community. This underlines Emanuel's (1973) view that 'narrowing gaps is a more difficult enterprise than bringing about progress as such . . . the latter is likely to be a more realistic objective' (p. 272).

Against this background it is appropriate to return to the relationship between non-spatial policies and regional development. In Chapter 3 it was argued that these policies, which include those for social security, education, health and defence, have added a major dimension to regional economies in the postwar period. The consequences have not been identical in all regions, but the general effects have been to generate stable employment, to raise demand in the form of private consumption and purchases by local and central government, and to contribute to more stable demand by redistributing income within and between regions via social security systems. Much remains to be done on the relationships between non-spatial policies and the amelioration of spatial economic problems but, returning briefly to the case of southern Belgium, their general significance can be readily demonstrated. Between 1959 and 1974 incentive-linked employment growth on the industrial estates did not exceed an average of 2,500 jobs per year and may have been as low as 2,000; yet between 1950 and 1970 public employment in southern Belgium (and primarily in the industrial centres) grew by 66,000 jobs, an annual average of 3,300. Moreover, much of the expansion complemented the rising socioeconomic aspirations of new elements in the labour force: 60 per cent of the growth was in education, with public administration and medical services providing virtually all the remainder (Vanhove and Klaassen, 1980). Quite apart from public sector employment creation, however, southern Belgium demonstrates the stabilising role of social security, which has been called upon to compensate for the fact that activity rates for men aged 45 or over are significantly lower than in the north of the country. Official regional statistics show that the discrepancy for the 55–59 age-group was no less than 10 per cent in the late 1970s and had worsened during the decade.

Although these observations relate to a single region, two official publications have emphasised the Community-wide importance of support mechanisms and public expenditure in general. One of the most important findings of the Mac-Dougall Report (Commission of the European Communities, 1977c) was that, in major regions, between half and two-thirds of the impact of cyclical fluctuations is offset by increased social benefits and by lower contributions to the exchequer. Equally significant was the conclusion that, on average, inter-regional income inequalities in the countries studied in the report were reduced by 40 per cent through all forms of public sector spending. More recently a major investigation into the impact of the 1970s recession on regional disparities has iden-tified an important distinction between trends in per capita disposable income and output (Commission of the European Communities, 1980a). Although disposable-income data, which include interregional social security transfers, are not available throughout the Community, the evidence suggests that only a marginal intensification occurred in interregional purchasing-power inequalities between 1970 and 1977. But interregional output trends, which exclude the transfer ele-ment, were strongly divergent, the ratio between per capita GDP in the ten strongest and ten weakest regions rising from 2·9:1 to 4·0:1 in the same period. Moreover, this clear deterioration in only the output dimension of the regional problem cannot be explained away in terms of expansion of the Community in 1973, for the investigation's statistical analysis shows almost identical trends in both the Six and the Nine.

There is, therefore, a strong case for regarding spatial and non-spatial policies as forces acting in parallel to ameliorate spatial prosperity contrasts, and it may be no exaggeration to claim that in some respects the effects of regional policies have been eclipsed in terms of scale and durability by the unobtru-sive progress of non-spatial programmes. However, in the early 1980s the scope for employing both types of policy to achieve more even development surfaces must be called into question. As recent OECD *Economic Surveys* have shown, in much of the Community the era of uninterrupted growth in non-spatial policies has ended and governments are taking increasingly critical views of the future exchequer implications of past public sector and welfare programmes. Meanwhile, recessional conditions have restricted regional policies by sharply curtailing the investment available to qualify for aid, and in many instances the value of regional assistance has been undermined by the introduction of industrial subsidies unencumbered by locational constraints. Conceptually it is useful to place these changes in the context of Kondratieff's theory that economic development is a long-wave phenomenon, powered by the emergence of leading activities which ultimately lose impetus, to be replaced by others after a period of uncertain quiescence (Kondratieff, 1936, repr. 1979; Kahn, 1979). The application of this theory in the European context is that the late 1960s and the 1970s witnessed the end of a long wave; and the extension of the argument is that the 1980s, and perhaps beyond, will be a period of great uncertainty in which the search is made for new propulsive forces and in which the future of many policies, including regional policy, must be reviewed.

Towards an Uncertain Future

Because regional policies, whatever progress they may have achieved, have clearly failed to provide protection from the reappearance of large-scale unemployment, it is natural that their future has been called into question (Pred, 1976; Mackay, 1979; Massey, 1979; Keeble, 1980). Is it now necessary to adopt defensive strategies based on maintaining rather than extending regional employment? In view of inner city decline and rising social tensions, should economic restructuring aim to rejuvenate cities rather than regions? Should regional programmes run parallel to other strategies designed to resuscitate 'growthmanship'? Or should they be rejected as once-promising experiments which often failed to meet early expectations? Answers to such questions are not clear-cut, but political considerations make rejection difficult and, as yet, the majority view is that the best way forward is to reappraise the suitability of present strategies for future needs. The OECD focused on this issue as early as 1974; most of the contributors to Maclennan and Parr (1979), touch on it; and the breadth of the debate may be outlined by considering the contrasting views of the revolutionary and evolutionary schools.

The revolutionary case is that existing regional policies are so ill-tuned to the control of capitalist forces that they must be replaced. This view is expressed most vehemently by Carney, Hudson and Lewis (1980), although Holland (1976a, 1976b, 1976c) is more cogent with respect to alternatives. The core of Holland's thesis is that postwar growth has favoured major 'meso-economic' industrial enterprises, which have stifled small-scale initiative and have become powerful enough to work against regional policy objectives. In seeking to harness this power the state may continue to offer incentives to these firms, but their economic resources and influence are such that it is necessary to devise and apply more effective influences on investment decisions. Major firms' investment programmes should therefore be submitted to governments and, if necessary, recast to conform with targets for problem regions; the progress of investment programmes should be carefully monitored to ensure that the spatial pattern of investment matches the agreed plan; and, to maximise returns on economic and social overhead capital, greater control should be exercised over intraregional locational choice. Realistically, it is recognised that the threat of tight control entails the danger of triggering the flight of capital, a natural reaction for multinational concerns already skilled in international financial manipulation. But it is argued that the withdrawal of capital can be contained, the key weapon being the threat of nationalisation. Thus the principal strategy advocated is that of far-reaching state control achieved through confrontation with big business and, if necessary, its coercion.

While not advocating the same policy, Massey (1979) has endorsed the view that present-day regional problems reflect the evolution of business organisation and capital's manipulation of space. Her conclusion is that, by concentrating low-skill functions in problem regions, major organisations have in effect created a new spatial division of labour. High-level functions, such as research and development, have normally been reserved for advanced regions, with the result that the problem of distributing high-level and low-level functions more equitably should be seen as an urgent policy issue.

Vanhove and Klaassen (1980) state the case for evolution on many fronts, which may be summarised under four main headings. *Co-ordination* must become a key activity for the Community, mainly to eliminate conflicts and contradictions arising from independently created national policies. To aid co-ordination, moves must be made to improve the 'transparency' of incentives so that their true value is known; responsibility for programme implementation should be clearly defined; and the Community itself should rationalise its currently fragmented aid systems through, for example, the creation of an economic and social development fund comprising the ERDF, the guidance section of the CAP and elements of the Social Fund. Community financial resources should be increased substantially, but *selectivity* should be exercised with respect to the projects and regions earmarked for priority investment. Scarce resources should be focused as far as possible on regions capable of achieving sustained growth, and from this proposal stems the politically controversial conclusion that 'in most cases priority should not be given to a country's least developed region' *Flexibility* is desirable because each problem region has its own development trajectory requiring action tailored to specific characteristics and needs; and the potential of tertiary and quaternary sectors should receive more serious consideration as a supplement to industrialisation. In the context of *innovative approaches* to stimulating development, three strategies receive special consideration. It is argued that the first, the provision of regional labour subsidies, would work against capital-intensity in a time of high unemployment, would be quick-acting and would lessen obstacles to Community monetary integration by creating, in effect, regional exchange-rate mechanisms. The second, the application of regional credit policies, would dampen cyclical fluctuations in the flow of investment finance to chosen development areas. (As was seen in Chapter 4, the core of a Community strategy of this type already exists in the spatial targeting policies for EIB and ECSC credit, but there is scope for expansion at both the national and international levels.) The third, the creation of a Community public sector with significant financial resources, would enable the Commission to inject income into weak regional economies without relying on private enterprise as an intermediary step in the process. This, too, would assist in counterbalancing cyclical fluctuations, but it is conceded that such a policy can only be a long-term objective, a conclusion which the MacDougall Report was also reluctantly forced to reach (Commission of the European Communities, 1977c).

Important though these and other strategic discussions are, as yet it is realistic to recognise that few practical steps have been taken towards the next phase of regional policy. As Yuill, Allen and Hull (1980) have commented, the 1970s did not see the emergence of a single major policy instrument; a recent official report on leader-region restrictions has concluded that it would be unwise to seek the introduction of a 'Eurocontrol' (Commission of the European Communities, 1980c); and the history of the ERDF has been one of fitful progress and frequent dilution in the interests of compromise. However, primarily because the recession has cast such a lengthy shadow over many regional policies and, indeed, over the future of the Community, a significant step appears imminent: the European Commission has been given the opportunity to reappraise the ERDF and argue for radical changes in the distribution of its aid. This opportunity was provided by the mandate of 30 May 1980, through which the Council of Ministers instructed the Commission to review Community policies against the current background of economic malaise and weak political impetus (Commission of the European Communities, 1981b). A new draft Regional Policy Regulation was sent to the Council in October 1981 and, although at the time of writing no decisions on the Commission's proposals have been announced, it seems probable that the political implications of severe recession will lead to significant changes in the ERDF's operations by the mid-1980s (Commission of the European Communities, 1981c).

With respect to expenditure strategy it is recognised that prospects for generating substantial employment flows into problem regions are worse than at any time in the postwar period. The new guidelines therefore give increased emphasis to harnessing a region's own development potential. In this respect they echo the EIB's strategy of directing assistance to small and medium-sized businesses, but the accent is not simply upon easing financial constraints which might restrict the development of such firms. The stated aim is to create productive jobs through the expansion of labour-intensive activities based on modern technology, the intention being to narrow the productivity gap at present separating rich and poor regions within the Community. It is now argued that to do this requires a more sophisticated approach than the provision of industrial grants, and a particular plea is made for the expansion of services whose weakness might undermine the expansion of small enterprises. These services include information dispersal, research facilities and technological assistance, but market studies would also qualify for aid, as would programmes to improve management effectiveness.

Several other proposals appear designed to shift the balance of political power in ERDF activities. For example, it is suggested that Community decision-making processes should be streamlined by transferring responsibility for grant decisions from the Council of Ministers to the Commission. Also, it is argued that regional and local authorities should participate fully in the preparation of programmes to attract aid from the Fund, in contrast to present practice which emphasises the relationships between governments and the Commission. To overcome the pitfall that expenditure on *ad hoc* projects may be wasteful, a further major proposal is that the Fund's quota aid should be provided through regional development contracts which would remain in force for several years. This is already the system for allocating non-quota aid, and its extension to the distribution of quota finance would be clearly related to the question of power over expenditure. Contracts would be awarded in accordance with defined regional programmes; by establishing national commitments these programmes should make it harder for governments to use ERDF finance to subsidise their efforts rather than augment them; and, by stressing the need to co-ordinate regional investment, the programme system would aim to tailor national policies to conform more closely with Community priorities. If, as is intended, the new ERDF Regulation gives legal force to the principle of co-ordination, there is little doubt that the

Commission's influence over policy formulation will increase significantly.

Acceptance of these proposals would not lead to an immediately obvious impact on assisted regions. Even in the long term their precise consequences are likely to prove debatable. Two other proposed developments, however, would have obvious repercussions, at least in the geographical distribution of aid. The first relates to the non-quota section of the ERDF which, it is proposed, should be increased from 5 to 20 per cent of available resources. Coupled with this expansion would be the freedom to concentrate assistance on 'areas in which the recession has caused decline in industry on an alarming scale'. This development would provide opportunities to aim investment more accurately at regions in urgent need of assistance, regions to be found in both the periphery and the core. The second development, in contrast, would disqualify the core from gaining assistance under the quota regulations, the section of the Fund with which the Commission has been most dissatisfied. Quota finance, distributed under the improved contract system described above, would instead be concentrated on the north-western and southern peripheries. Ireland and the UK would receive slightly more than a third of the allocations, with Greece and, most particularly, the Mezzogiorno accounting for almost all the remainder (Table 5.1).

Table 5.1 *Commission Proposals for Revised ERDF Quotas, August 1981*

	Proposed share (%)
Ireland	7·31
UK (Northern Ireland and parts of Scotland, Wales, North and North West England)	29·28
Italy (Mezzogiorno)	43·67
Greece (excluding Athens and Thessaloniki)	15·97
Denmark (Greenland)	1·30
France (Overseas Departments)	2·47
	100·00

Source: Commission of the European Communities, 1981c.

Once again, if this new framework is accepted it will represent a notable Commission victory, this time in its attempt to subdue the claims of the core in favour of the periphery.

From the Commission's viewpoint the argument that a selection of peripheral regions should receive clearly preferential treatment is substantiated by the findings of the *Regions of Europe* report (Commission of the European Communities, 1980a). Combining the criteria of per capita GDP exchange rates and long-term unemployment into an index, this report demonstrated that the priority regions in Table 5.1 all score less than 75, against the Community average of 100. Bearing in mind the troubled history of the Fund, this quantified approach to the evaluation of regional backwardness may prove to be an invaluable lever in the decision-making process. In addition, fresh evidence strengthening the Commission's case has come with the publication of a report by Keeble, Owens and Thompson (1981) concerning centrality, peripherality and the relative development of regions. In this investigation each region's output was related to output and accessibility in the Community's entire set of regions, the outcome being a measure of regional economic potential expressed in EUAs per km. By themselves the figures underline core–periphery contrasts, as the averages of member states' regional scores demonstrate (Table 5.2). But a more significant point is that correlation and regression analyses forming the core of the investigation demonstrate that, in the Community as a whole, many indicators of economic health move in sympathy with the regional economic potential variable. It is true that the strength of the relationships identified must not be overstated: only seventeen of the forty-seven analyses produced correlation coefficients of 0·45 or above, and ten results were too weak to be statistically significant. However, the fact that an economic criterion is influenced, if only to a minor degree, by relative location is significant: when thirty-seven such relationships are identified the argument that regional economic health is a partial function of location becomes particularly strong. As Keeble, Owens and Thompson conclude (p. 185), 'a complex of inter-related economic characteristics . . . in combination render the inhabitants and firms of the Community's peripheral regions economically significantly disadvantaged, relative to their counterparts in the central regions'. From the Commission's

Table 5.2   *Regional Economic Potential Relative to the Community as a Whole, 1977*

	No. of regions evaluated	Regional scores (EUAm/km)		
		average	maximum	minimum
Belgium	9	5,230·9	6,349·2	4,186·1
Netherlands	11	4,777·5	6,389·7	3,236·3
West Germany	34	4,368·2	9,664·1	3,118·0
Luxembourg	1	4,234·6	—	—
France	22	3,364·0	7,346·6	1,634·0
United Kingdom	11	3,104·7	4,951·4	1,614·9
Denmark	3	2,667·4	3,329·1	2,304·4
Italy	20	2,158·3	3,823·0	1,134·3
Ireland	1	1,686·6	—	—
Spain[a]	13	1,458·0	1,848·6	1,070·4
Portugal[a]	4	1,131·6	1,223·7	1,030·3
Greece[a]	9	913·3	1,300·8	679·7

Note: a Calculated on the basis of a Community of Twelve. Recalculation of the figures for the Nine on this basis leads to very marginal changes.

Source: Calculated from Keeble, Owens and Thompson, 1981, table 3.5 and app. C.

viewpoint this finding, the principal outcome of a Community-funded research project, could not have been published at a more appropriate moment.

Whatever form future regional policies take, it is clear that they must recognise that the Community is exposed to global forces which are creating a new economic climate (Dahrendorf, 1982). Outstanding amongst these is the emergence since the 1950s of the 'new international division of labour', the reorientation of major industries away from traditional producing countries as production opportunities and advantages have been perceived elsewhere (Fröbel, Heinrichs and Kreye, 1977, 1980). Within the Community this force has affected traditional industries (such as steel, textiles, clothing and shipbuilding) as well as much more recent leading activities (notably car manufacturing). It cannot be anticipated that these activities will return to former output and employment levels as 'normal' recessional conditions abate and, as Oakey (1981) has shown, industry as a whole must adapt to the impact of technological change, with its far-reaching implications for development strategies based on labour absorption.

These considerations suggest that Vanhove and Klaassen

(1980) and Marquand (1980b) are correct in arguing that more attention should be given to the economic restructuring potential of non-manufacturing activities. Yet the alternatives are not without drawbacks. Agriculture and mining are now minor Community employers and, even where they are regionally important, development programmes are likely to shun labour-intensity. Tourism, in contrast, will probably remain labour-intensive and can form the basis of development plans if finance is available; but continued expansion will depend on prosperity levels, only a few regions can exploit tourism to the full, seasonality remains marked, and there are problems of sensitivity to increased global competition for the tourist market. (In this connection air transport has ensured that the new international division of labour has implications extending beyond manufacturing.) Technological innovation, it is true, may greatly increase the technical feasibility of private and public sector office decentralisation in the immediate future, yet this potential freedom may experience powerful countervailing forces. Leader-region employers no longer face the worst problems of overstressed labour markets, and trade unions have already hardened opposition to the loss of employment through relocation.

Despite the great uncertainty surrounding the nature of appropriate future policies, in conclusion it must be recognised that the European Commission's commitment to the diminution of deep-seated spatial economic disparities remains undiminished. In part this reflects the desire for greater social justice, but there is also a basic political motivation: even more than in the past, regional inequality is seen to be an impediment to Community integration and, therefore, to the emergence of a truly cohesive power bloc. But this commitment to regional policy for social and political ends, which is advanced in many Community publications, is itself threatened by the implications of a second major policy with political overtones – Community expansion. To a great extent both the first enlargement and the current expansion phase were undertaken with the aim of increasing the number of nations locked together in such a way that the geographical limits of common interest and outlook were permanently extended. Yet the first enlargement intensified the peaks and troughs of the Community's development surface, magnified the challenge facing regional policy and, according to the Commission's argument concerning the political significance of regional disparities, decreased the probability of achieving political cohesion. As was indicated in Chapter 2, in a much more difficult economic climate the 1980s will witness an accentuated repetition of this sequence on the Community's southern periphery, the danger being that the North/South polarisation of attitudes will generate confrontation and the threat of political fragmentation. Thus the inevitable increase in internal development contrasts has the potential to sap the political stability of the Community, a conclusion which once again points to the need to improve the efficiency of spatial policy. Only time will tell whether more impressive progress towards this elusive goal can be achieved.

Bibliography

This bibliography details works referred to in the text, but it is selective in the sense that the literature on European regional development is too extensive to be listed exhaustively. Readers will find, therefore, that most of the items quoted below have substantial reference lists which may be used to explore the subject more deeply. Where appropriate, references have been annotated to clarify their subject matter, summarise their arguments, or draw attention to related items.

Aldcroft, D. H. (1978), *The European Economy 1914–1970* (London, Croom Helm). An introduction to major development trends, supported by a substantial bibliography.

Armstrong, W. H. (1979), 'Community regional policy: a survey and critique', *Regional Studies*, vol. 12, pp. 511–28.

Ashcroft, B. and Taylor, J. (1979), 'The effect of regional policy on the movement of manufacturing industry in Great Britain', in *Regional Policy: Past Experience and New Directions*, ed. D. Maclennan and J. B. Parr (Oxford: Martin Robertson), pp. 43–64. Although concerned with Britain rather than Europe, this book raises many important questions with respect to strategies for regional development.

Barzanti, S. (1965), *The Underdeveloped Areas within the Common Market* (Princeton, NJ: Princeton University Press). A study focusing on the development problems of Italy and south-west France.

Bennett, R. J. (1980), *The Geography of Public Finance* (London and New York: Methuen). A broad consideration of public finance in advanced economies which touches upon the Community and Community members in several places.

Brooke, M. Z. (1977), 'The multinational company in Europe', in *Government, Business and Labour in European Capitalism*, ed. R. T. Griffiths (London: Europotentials Press), pp. 89–104. The book as a whole provides insights into the general economic environment in which inter-regional competition operates.

Brown, A. J. (1972), *The Framework of Regional Economics in the United Kingdom* (Cambridge: Cambridge University Press). A wide-ranging survey of regional development processes and an evaluation of policy effects in Britain.

Brownrigg, M. (1980), 'Industrial contraction and the regional multiplier effect: an application in Scotland', *Town Planning Review*, vol. 51, pp. 195–210.

Buck, T. W. and Atkins, M. H. (1976), 'The impact of British regional

11>

policies on employment growth', *Oxford Economic Papers*, vol. 28, pp. 118–32.

Burtenshaw, D. (1976a), 'Problems of frontier regions in the EEC', in *Economy and Society in the EEC: Spatial Perspectives*, ed. R. Lee and P. E. Ogden (Farnborough: Saxon House), pp. 217–32. The book as a whole provides an introduction to a wide range of Community development trends and problems.

Burtenshaw, D. (1976b), *Saar-Lorraine* (London: Oxford University Press).

Camina, M. M. (1974), 'Local authorities and the attraction of industry', *Progress in Planning*, vol. 3, pp. 85–182. A survey covering, among other things, the provision of facilities, promotion policies and their effects.

Cao-Pinna, V. (1974), 'Regional policy in Italy', in *Public Policy and Regional Economic Development*, ed. N. M. Hansen (Cambridge, Mass.: Ballinger), pp. 137–80. Other chapters provide comparisons with experience elsewhere in Europe and in North America.

Carney, J., Hudson, R., and Lewis, J. (1980), *Regions in Crisis* (London: Croom Helm).

Chenery, H. B. (1962), 'Development policies for southern Italy', *Quarterly Journal of Economics*, vol. 76, pp. 515–47. This paper is reprinted on pp. 198–236 of *Regional Analysis*, ed. L. Needleman (Harmondsworth: Penguin, 1968), a collection of contributions exploring the theory and practice of regional development.

Claval, P. (1975), 'Contemporary human geography in France', *Progress in Geography*, vol. 7, pp. 255–92. Pages 269–73 of this lengthy paper are particularly relevant to the theme considered here.

Clout, H. D. (1981), *Regional Development in Western Europe* (Chichester: Wiley).

Collins, D. (1975), *The European Communities: The Social Policy of the First Phase, Vol. 1, The European Coal and Steel Community 1951–70* (London: Martin Robertson).

Commission of the European Communities (1971), *Regional Development in the Community: Analytical Survey* (Brussels: Commission of the European Communities). This factual investigation can usefully be read in conjunction with the Commission's report *The Regions of Europe* (1980); see below.

Commission of the European Communities (1973), *Report on Regional Problems in the Enlarged Community* (Brussels: Commission of the European Communities).

Commission of the European Communities (1976), *Competition Report, 1975* (Brussels: Commission of the European Communities).

Commission of the European Communities (1977a), 'Community regional policy: new guidelines', *Bulletin of the European Communities*, Supplement 2/77. A detailed document revealing the Commission's mid-1970s attitude to regional strategy. The specific issue of assisted region definition is on p. 28.

Commission of the European Communities (1977b), *Multinational Companies in the European Community* (Luxembourg: Commission of the European Communities).

Commission of the European Communities (1977c), *Report on the Role of*

Public Financing in European Integration (Brussels: Commission of the European Communities). A two-volume work, commonly known as the MacDougall Report, providing a general overview (Vol. 1) based on specific surveys (Vol. 2).

Commission of the European Communities (1978), *Regional Aid Systems: Principles of Coordination*, COM Document 636 Final (Brussels: Commission of the European Communities).

Commission of the European Communities (1979a), *The Second Enlargement of the European Community* (Luxembourg: Office for Official Publications of the European Communities). A policy statement summarising the findings of Supplements 1, 2, 3, 5 and 9 of the *Bulletin of the European Communities* (1978).

Commission of the European Communities (1979b), *The Regional Development Programmes*, Regional Policy Series, No. 17 (Brussels: Commission of the European Communities). A companion volume, *Regional Incentives in the European Community*, appeared as No. 15 in the series in 1979.

Commission of the European Communities (1979c), *Regional Development Programmes: Belgium 1978–1980*, Regional Policy Series, No. 14 (Brussels: Commission of the European Communities). A detailed study of background, policy goals, financial resources and policy implementation, a format followed by other national volumes in the series.

Commission of the European Communities (1980a), *The Regions of Europe: First Periodic Report on the Social and Economic Situation in the Regions of the Community*, COM Document (80) 816 Final. A major report on recent trends in interregional disparities, also published in 1981 by the Commission under the same title in a format similar to that of the Regional Policy Series.

Commission of the European Communities (1980b), *Social Indicators* (Luxembourg: Eurostat).

Commission of the European Communities (1980c), *Deglommeration Policy in the European Community*, Regional Policy Series, No. 18 (Brussels: Commission of the European Communities).

Commission of the European Communities (1981a), *Fourteenth General Report* (Brussels: Commission of the European Communities). Several sections of this annual publication relate to regional policy, instruments and aid agencies.

Commission of the European Communities (1981b), *Bulletin of the European Communities*, Supplement 1/81. A broad policy statement following the mandate of 30 May 1980. See also Supplement 4/81.

Commission of the European Communities (1981c), *Bulletin of the European Communities*, vol. 14, no. 10, pp. 8–10. For additional information on reform of the ERDF in the early 1980s see the *Bulletin*, vol. 14, nos 7/8.

Commission of the European Communities (forthcoming), *Les Travailleurs frontaliers en Europe*. This report will appear as No. 9 in the Regional Policy Series (see below) but publication has been delayed.

Commission of the European Communities, Regional Policy series. The principal series used by the Commission to disseminate information on national policies and views on regional development issues.

Crompton, D., Barlow, A. T., and Downing, S. (1976), *Component Sup-*

pliers to the Car Industry (Birmingham: Department of Industry). Copies of this report are available direct from the Department of Industry.

Dahrendorf, R. (ed.) (1982), *European Economies in Crisis* (London: Weidenfeld & Nicolson).

Department of Industry (1981), 'Methodology for measuring the effects and costs of regional incentives', in *Minutes of Evidence Taken Before the Public Accounts Committee, March 4 and 9, 1981* (London: HMSO). The Department's statement is followed by an interesting cross-examination of witnesses and an appendix with data on IDC refusals.

Deubner, C. (1980), 'The southern enlargement of the European Community: opportunities and dilemmas from a West German point of view', *Journal of Common Market Studies*, vol. 18, pp. 229–45.

Dickinson, R. E. (1947), *City, Region and Regionalism* (London: Routledge & Kegan Paul). Revised and published as *City and Region* (1964), with an abridged version, *The City Region in Western Europe*, following in 1967.

Downs, R. M., and Stea, D. (1977), *Image and Environment: Cognitive Mapping and Spatial Behavior* (London: Edward Arnold).

Dubey, V. (1964), 'The definition of regional economics', *Journal of Regional Science*, vol. 5, pp. 25–9. Reprinted in a useful reader on regional development: *Regional Economics*, ed. D. L. McKee, R. D. Dean and W. H. Leahy (London: Collier Macmillan, 1970), pp. 3–8.

EIB (1978), *The European Investment Bank 1958—1978* (Luxembourg: European Investment Bank).

EIB *Annual Report*. Monitors general economic trends, surveys the evolution of EIB strategy and reports loan allocations in some detail.

EIB *Information*. A periodic publication available in six languages; provides surveys of general and specific policy issues.

Emanuel, A. (1973), *Issues of Regional Policy* (Paris: Organisation for Economic Co-operation and Development).

ERDF *Annual Report*. The utility of this survey has increased considerably as the Fund's activities have expanded.

European Parliament (1960), *Regional Policy Problems and Means of Implementing such a Policy in a Community of the Six* (Strasbourg: Economic and Financial Committee).

European Parliament (1963), *Rapport sur la politique régionale dans la Communauté* (Strasbourg: Economic and Financial Committee).

European Parliament (1966), *Rapport sur la première communication de la Commission de la CEE sur la politique régionale dans la CEE* (Strasbourg: Economic and Financial Committee).

Eversley, D. C. (1972), 'Rising costs and static incomes: some economic consequences of regional planning in London', *Urban Studies*, vol. 9, pp. 347–68.

Ferreira, A. da Silva (1978), 'The economics of enlargement: trade effects on the applicant countries', *Journal of Common Market Studies*, vol. 17, pp. 120–41.

Frederiksson, C. G., and Lindmark, G. (1979), 'From firms to systems of firms: a study of interregional dependence in a dynamic society', in *Industrial Systems*, ed. F. E. I. Hamilton and G. J. R. Linge (Chichester: Wiley), pp. 155–80.

Friedmann, J. (1966), *Regional Development Policy: A Case Study of Venezuela* (Cambridge, Mass.: MIT Press). A work which directly or indirectly influenced policy formulators in many parts of the world.

Friedmann, J. (1972), 'A general theory of polarised development', in *Growth Centres in Regional Economic Development*, ed. N. M. Hansen (New York: The Free Press).

Fröbel, F., Heinrichs, J. and Kreye, O. (1977), 'The tendency towards a New International Division of Labour', *Review* [sic], vol. 1, pp. 73–88. Sections following p. 79 are particularly informative.

Fröbel, F., Heinrichs, J., and Kreye, O. (1980), *The New International Division of Labour* (London and Paris: Cambridge University Press and Editions de la Maison des Sciences de l'Homme). An extended treatment of issues raised by the authors' 1977 paper.

Gillet, M. (1969), 'The coal age and the rise of coalfields in the North and the Pas-de-Calais', in *Essays in European Economic History 1789–1914*, ed. F. Crouzet, W. H. Chaloner and W. M. Stern (London: Edward Arnold), pp. 179–202.

Gold, J. R. (1980), *An Introduction to Behavioural Geography* (Oxford: Oxford University Press).

Gordon, R. L. (1970), *The Evolution of Energy Policy in Western Europe: The Reluctant Retreat from Coal* (New York, Praeger).

Gould, P. R., and White, R. (1974), *Mental Maps* (Harmondsworth: Penguin).

Graziani, A. (1978), 'The Mezzogiorno in the Italian economy', *Cambridge Journal of Economics*, vol. 2, pp. 355–72. An important survey of theories relating to the Mezzogiorno's problems, together with a critical analysis of traditional industrialisation policy.

Green, H. D. (1977), 'Industrialists' information levels of regional incentives', *Regional Studies*, vol. 11, pp. 7–18.

Guttenberg, A. Z. (1977), 'Classifying regions: a conceptual approach', *International Regional Science Review*, vol. 2, pp. 1–14. Despite its North American orientation, this paper offers concepts widely applicable elsewhere.

Hall, P. G. (1974), *Urban and Regional Planning* (Harmondsworth: Penguin). Although mainly concerned with British experience, the book touches on Europe, especially in chapter 8.

Hamilton, F. E. I. (1976), 'Multinational enterprise and the European Economic Community', *Tijdschrift voor Economische en Sociale Geografie*, vol. 67, pp. 258–78. Reprinted in *Industrial Change*, ed. F. E. I. Hamilton (London: Longman, 1978), pp. 24–41.

Hare, P. G. (1977), The effects of regional policy on employment: problems of theory and measurement', in *Government, Business and Labour in European Capitalism*, ed. R. T. Griffiths (London: Europotentials Press), pp. 169–86.

Hartshorne, R. (1939), *The Nature of Geography* (Lancaster, Penn.: Association of American Geographers). Chapters 8 and 9 provide lengthy consideration of regional concepts.

Hirschman, A. O. (1958), *The Strategy of Economic Development* (Englewood

Cliffs, NJ: Prentice-Hall). Pages 183–201 are particularly useful with respect to theory and are reproduced in *Regional Economics*, ed. D. L. McKee, R. D. Dean and W. H. Leahy (London: Collier Macmillan, 1970) pp. 105–20.

HMSO (1980), 'Employment in the public sector', *Economic Progress Report*, no. 118, pp. 4–6.

Holland, S. (ed.) (1972), *The State as Entrepreneur* (London:Weidenfeld & Nicolson). A detailed examination of the Italian Institute for Industrial Reconstruction (IRI).

Holland, S. (1976a), *Capital Versus the Regions* (London: Macmillan).

Holland, S. (1976b), *The Regional Problem* (London: Macmillan).

Holland, S. (1976c), 'Meso-economics, multinational capital and regional inequality', in *Economy and Society in the EEC: Spatial Perspectives*, ed. R. Lee and P. E. Ogden (Farnborough: Saxon House), pp. 38–62. The book as a whole introduces a wide range of Community development trends and problems.

House, J. W. (1978), *France: An Applied Geography* (London: Methuen).

House of Commons Expenditure Committee (1972), 'Regional development incentives', *Parliamentary Papers*, Session 1972–3, vol. 24, pp. 1–524. Apart from the comment quoted in the text, this volume contains a wealth of evidence on British aid, including many statements by major firms revealing their perceptions of incentives.

Husain, M. S. (1981), 'Influences on development policy in the Port of Hamburg', in *Cityport Industrialization: Spatial Analysis and Planning Strategies*, ed. B. S. Hoyle and D. A. Pinder (Oxford: Pergamon), pp. 223–42.

Jarrett, R. J. (1975), 'Disincentives: the other side of regional development policy', *Journal of Common Market Studies*, vol. 13, pp. 379–90.

Kahn, H. (1979), *World Economic Development* (London: Croom Helm).

Keeble, D. E. (1976), *Industrial Location and Planning in the United Kingdom* (London: Methuen).

Keeble, D. E. (1980), 'Industrial decline, regional policy and the urban–rural manufacturing shift in the United Kingdom', *Environment and Planning A*, vol. 12, pp. 945–62.

Keeble, D., Owens P. L., and Thompson, C. (1981), *The Influence of Peripheral and Central Locations on the Relative Development of Regions* (Cambridge: Department of Geography, Cambridge University). It is expected that a version of this report will be published by the European Community, a co-sponsor of the investigation.

Keynes, J. M. (1936) *The General Theory of Employment, Interest and Money* (London: Macmillan).

King, L. J., and Clarke, G. L. (1978), 'Government policy and regional development', *Progress in Human Geography*, vol. 2, pp. 1–16. A broad review, including a section on evaluation issues.

King, R. (1976), 'The evolution of international labour migration movements concerning the EEC', *Tijdschrift voor Economische en Sociale Geografie*, vol. 67, pp. 66–82.

Klaassen, L. H. (1968), *Social Amenities in Area Economic Growth* (Paris: Organisation for Economic Co-operation and Development). Klaassen also touches upon social infrastructure in *Area Economic and Social Redevelopment*, again published by the OECD (1965).

Kondratieff, N. D. (1936, repr. 1979), 'The long waves of economic life', *Review* [*sic*], vol. 4, pp. 519–62. The 1936 paper was an incomplete translation from the original German. The omissions were rectified in the 1979 version, which appeared with a collection of papers and a bibliography examining the basic theory.

Lasuén, J. R. (1974), 'Spain's regional growth', in *Public Policy and Regional Economic Development*, ed. N. M. Hansen (Cambridge, Mass.: Ballinger), pp. 235–70. Other chapters provide comparison with experience elsewhere in Europe and in North America.

Law, D. (1975), 'The economic problems of Ireland, Scotland and Wales', in *Economic Sovereignty and Regional Policy*, ed. J. Vaizey (Dublin: Gill & Macmillan), pp. 233–54. The book as a whole provides useful background on theory, Community expansion and the effects of spatial and non-spatial policies.

Lawson, R., and Reed, B. (1975), *Social Security in the European Community* (London: Chatham House/PEP).

Leigh, R., and North, D. (1978), 'Acquisitions in British industries: implications for regional development', in *Contemporary Industrialization*, ed. F. E. I. Hamilton (London: Longman), pp. 158–81. The same authors cover similar ground in *Regional Studies*, vol. 12, 1978, pp. 227–46.

Licari, J. (1970), 'The European Investment Bank', *Journal of Common Market Studies*, vol. 8, pp. 192–215.

Lind, H., and Flockton, C. (1970), *Regional Policy in Britain and the Six* (London: Chatham House/PEP).

Mackay, R. (1976), 'The impact of the Regional Employment Premium', in *The Economics of Industrial Subsidies*, ed. A. Whiting (London: HMSO), pp. 225–42. The remainder of the book examines many other facets of British incentive strategy.

Mackay, R. (1979), 'The death of regional policy – or resurrection squared?', *Regional Studies*, vol. 13, pp. 281–95.

Maclennan, D., and Parr, J. B. (eds) (1979), *Regional Policy: Past Experience and New Directions* (Oxford: Martin Robertson). Although concerned with Britain rather than Europe, this book raises many important questions with respect to regional development strategies.

Marquand, J. (1980a), 'Change and divergence in the EEC', *Journal of Common Market Studies*, vol. 19, pp. 1–20. A paper arguing the power of divergence tendencies in comparison with regional policy.

Marquand, J. (1980b), *The Role of Tertiary Activities in Regional Policy*, Regional Policy Series, No. 19 (Brussels: Commission of the European Communities).

Mason, C. M. (1981), 'Industrial promotion advertising', *Town and Country Planning*, vol. 50, pp. 134–6.

Massey, D. (1979), 'In what sense a regional problem?' *Regional Studies*, vol. 13, pp. 233–43. A paper which sets out to challenge, in the British context, a number of widely held assumptions relating to regional policy and problems.

Maunder, P. (ed.) (1979), *Government Intervention in the Developed Economy*

(London, Croom Helm). Three chapters examine in depth the UK, West Germany and France, while the remainder provide comparisons with Sweden, the USA, Australia and Japan.

Maynard, A. (1975), *Health Care in the European Community* (London: Croom Helm).

McCrone, G. (1969), 'Regional policy in the European Communities', in *Economic Integration in Europe*, ed. G. R. Denton (London: Weidenfeld & Nicolson), pp. 194–219. Many other contributions to this volume examine issues related to the spatial distribution of growth.

McCrone, G. (1975), 'The determinants of regional growth rates', in *Economic Sovereignty and Regional Policy*, ed. J. Vaizey (Dublin: Gill & Macmillan), pp. 63–79. McCrone provides some theory, and emphasises structural factors, as well as locational ones, in the emergence of regional problems.

McHale, V. E., and Shaber, S. (1976), 'Reflections on the political economy of regional development in Western Europe', *Journal of Common Market Studies*, vol. 14, pp. 180–98.

Meyer, J. R. (1963), 'Regional economics: a survey', *American Economic Review*, vol. 53, pp. 19–54. Reprinted in *Regional Analysis*, ed. L. Needleman (Harmondsworth: Penguin, 1968), pp. 19–60.

Milward, A., and Saul, S. B. (1977), *The Development of the Economies of Continental Europe* (London: Allen and Unwin).

Molle, W., Van Holst, B., and Smit, H. (1980), *Regional Disparity and Economic Development in the European Community* (Farnborough: Saxon House). Disparities are identified and evaluated according to a variety of socioeconomic indicators.

Moore, B., and Rhodes, J. (1975), 'The economic and exchequer implications of British regional economic policy', in *Economic Sovereignty and Regional Policy*, ed. J. Vaizey (Dublin: Gill & Macmillan), pp. 80–102. The same authors have put forward very similar optimistic arguments elsewhere; see House of Commons Expenditure Committee (1972) above.

Moore, B., and Rhodes, J. (1976a), 'Regional economic policy and the movement of manufacturing firms to Development Areas', *Economica*, vol. 43, pp. 17–31.

Moore, B., and Rhodes, J. (1976b), 'A quantitative analysis of the effects of the Regional Employment Premium and other regional policy instruments', in *The Economics of Industrial Subsidies*, ed. A. Whiting (London: HMSO), pp. 191–219. The remainder of the book examines many other facets of British incentive strategy.

Myrdal, G. (1957), *Economic Theory and Underdeveloped Regions* (London: Duckworth).

Nicol, W. R. (1979), 'Relaxation and reorientation: parallel trends in regional disincentive policies', *Urban Studies*, vol. 16, pp. 333–9.

Nocifora, E. (1978), 'Poles of development and the southern question: the literature on industrialization in the Italian South since the Second World War', *International Journal of Urban and Regional Research*, vol. 2, pp. 361–78.

Oakey, R.P. (1981), *High Technology Industry and Industrial Location* (Aldershot: Gower). Although concerned with one high-technology industry in

Britain, this investigation raises important general questions relating to technological change and unemployment.

OECD (1974), *Reappraisal of Regional Policies in OECD Countries* (Paris: Organisation for Economic Co-operation and Development).

OECD *Economic Surveys* (Paris: Organisation for Economic Co-operation and Development). Periodic reports on the economies of OECD members with critical evaluations of recent trends.

O'Farrell, P. N. (1978), 'An analysis of new industry location: the Irish case', *Progress in Planning*, vol. 9, pp. 129–229. An investigation primarily based on statistical analysis of responses to a survey of investors in the Republic.

Official Journal of the European Communities. Commission decisions and new Community regulations, etc., are promulgated via the *Journal* at frequent intervals throughout the year.

Paine, S. H. (1977), 'The changing role of migrant workers in the advanced capitalist economies of Western Europe', in *Government, Business and Labour in European Capitalism*, ed. R. T. Griffiths (London: Europotentials Press), pp. 199–225. In addition to surveying the role of migrants in Europe, Paine argues that the era of large-scale labour movements is now over, with far-reaching implications for countries which previously relied on the export of labour.

Perroux, F. (1950), 'Economic space: theory and applications', *Quarterly Journal of Economics*, vol. 64, pp. 89–104.

Perroux, F. (1955), 'Note sur la notion de pôle de croissance', *Economie appliquée*. This paper appears in an English translation in *Regional Economics*, ed. D. L. McKee, R. D. Dean and W. H. Leahy (London: Collier Macmillan, 1970), pp. 93–103.

Pinder, D. A. (1976), *The Netherlands* (Folkestone: Dawson). An industrial geography, the first half of which is concerned with development trends, spatial imbalance and regional policies.

Pinder, D. A. (1978), 'Guiding economic development in the EEC: the approach of the European Investment Bank', *Geography*, vol. 63, pp. 88–97. A review of the temporal and spatial evolution of the Bank's strategy and its relationship with development theory.

Pinder, D. A. (1981), 'Community attitude as a limiting factor in port growth: the case of Rotterdam', in *Cityport Industrialization and Regional Development: Spatial Analysis and Planning Strategies*, ed. B. S. Hoyle and D. A. Pinder (Oxford: Pergamon), pp. 181–99. The paper argues that a policy of industrial concentration and port expansion caused a revolution in attitudes towards the development of the southern Randstad.

Pitfield, D. E. (1978), 'The quest for effective regional policy', *Regional Studies*, vol. 12, pp. 429–43. Further evidence relating to early policy in Britain has been provided by A. A. Lonie and H. M. Begg in *Regional Studies*, vol. 13, 1979, pp. 497–500.

Pred, A. R. (1967), 'Behaviour and location: foundations for a geographic and dynamic location theory', *Lund Studies in Geography*, Series B, nos 27 and 28.

Pred, A. R. (1976), 'The inter-urban transmission of growth in advanced economies: empirical findings versus regional planning assumptions',

Regional Studies, vol. 10, pp. 151–71. Although based on American experience, this paper is useful for its challenge to the validity of growth centres as regional development instruments and for its plea that regional policy should increasingly look to the tertiary sector to create employment.

Prud'homme, R. (1974), 'Regional economic policy in France, 1962–1972', in *Public Policy and Regional Economic Development*, ed. N. M. Hansen (Cambridge, Mass.: Ballinger), pp. 33–64. Other chapters provide comparison with experience elsewhere in Europe and in North America.

Rees, M. (1973), *The Public Sector in the Mixed Economy* (London: Batsford). A review of central and local government expenditure, the activities of public corporations and state shareholdings.

Richardson, H. W. (1975), *Regional Development Policy and Planning in Spain* (Farnborough: Saxon House).

Richardson, H. W. (1978a), 'The state of regional economics', *International Regional Science Review*, vol. 3, pp. 1–48. The final third of this paper comprises an extensive thematic bibliography.

Richardson, H. W. (1978b), *Regional and Urban Economics* (Harmondsworth: Penguin).

Riley, R. C. (1976), *Belgium* (Folkestone: Dawson). An industrial geography, the first part of which examines development trends, regional disequilibrium and regional policies.

Riley, R. C., and Smith, J. L. (1981), 'Industrialization in naval ports: the Portsmouth case', in *Cityport Industrialization and Regional Development: Spatial Analysis and Planning Strategies*, ed. B. S. Hoyle and D. A. Pinder (Oxford: Pergamon), pp. 133–50. A detailed examination of the navy's domination of a local economy and of the process of readjustment towards a more typical economy.

Romus, P. (1975), 'Regional policy in the European Community', in *Economic Sovereignty and Regional Policy*, ed. J. Vaizey (Dublin: Gill & Macmillan), pp. 122–32. The paper underlines the complexities of national policies and argues for their rationalisation and for co-ordination at the national level.

Salt, J., and Clout, H. (eds) (1976), *Migration in Post-war Europe* (London: Oxford University Press). This book offers the most comprehensive overview of the migration phenomenon at present available.

Sant, M. E. (1975), *Industrial Movement and Regional Development* (Oxford: Pergamon).

Scargill, D. I. (ed.), Problem Regions of Europe series (London: Oxford University Press). A series of short investigations of specific regions drawn from many parts of Europe.

Schofield, J. A. (1976), 'Economic efficiency and regional policy', *Urban Studies*, vol. 13, pp. 181–92.

Schofield, J. A. (1979), 'Macro-evaluations of the impact of regional policy in Britain: a review of regional research', *Urban Studies*, vol. 16, pp. 251–71.

Seers, D., Schaffer, B. and Kiljunen, M. (eds) (1979), *Underdeveloped Europe: Studies in Core–Periphery Relations* (Hassocks: Harvester). Major sections are devoted to general issues, population and capital movements, the southern periphery and north-western periphery.

Sheahan, J. B. (1976), 'Experience with public enterprise in France and Italy', in *Public Enterprise: Economic Analysis of Theory and Practice*, ed. W. G. Shepherd (Lexington, Mass.: D. C. Heath/Lexington Books), pp. 123–83. A detailed account of the extent of nationalisation, together with a critical appraisal of progress and an evaluation of nationalisation in the development programme for the Mezzogiorno.

Shlaim, A., and Yannopoulos, G. N. (eds) (1976), *The EEC and the Mediterranean Countries* (Cambridge: Cambridge University Press). A collection of essays, many suggesting that the development of the Community Mediterranean policy has been haphazard and that the benefits of polarisation towards the Nine are likely to outweigh the impact of trickling down in the Mediterranean countries.

Short, J. (1978), 'The regional distribution of public expenditure in Great Britain', *Regional Studies*, vol. 12, pp. 499–510.

Stabler, J. C. (1968), 'Exports and evolution: the process of regional change', *Land Economics*, vol. 49, pp. 11–23. Reprinted in *Regional Economics*, ed. D. L. Mckee, R. D. Dean and W. H. Leahy (London: Collier Macmillan, 1970), pp. 49–64.

Streit, M. E. (1977), 'Government and business: the case of West Germany', in *Government, Business and Labour in European Capitalism*, ed. R. T. Griffiths (London: Europotentials Press), pp. 120–34.

Talbot, R. B. (1978), 'The European Community's Regional Fund', *Progress in Planning*, vol. 8, pp. 183–281. A very detailed and well-documented investigation of hesitant progress towards the creation of the Fund.

Thirlwall, A. P. (1974), 'Regional economic disparities and regional policy in the Common Market', *Urban Studies*, vol. 11, pp. 1–12. A paper stressing the handicaps imposed on regional policy by the pursuit of Common Market policies.

Thoman, G. R. (1973), *Foreign Investment and Regional Development: The Theory and Practice of Investment Incentives, with a Case Study of Belgium* (New York: Praeger).

Tuppen, J. N. (1978), 'A geographical appraisal of transfrontier commuting in Western Europe: the example of Alsace', *International Migration Review*, vol. 12, pp. 386–404.

Tuppen, J. N. (1980), *France* (Folkestone: Dawson). An industrial geography which gives considerable attention to regional disequilibria and spatial policy issues.

Vanhove, N., and Klaassen, L. H. (1980), *Regional Policy: A European Approach* (Farnborough: Saxon House). A wide-ranging investigation of problems, causes, policies and possible future policies at the national and Community levels.

Wallace, H. (1977), 'The establishment of the Regional Development Fund: common policy or pork barrel?', in *Policy-making in the European Communities*, ed. H. Wallace, W. Wallace and C. Webb (London: Wiley), pp. 137–63.

Wallace, W., and Edwards, G. (1976), *A Wider European Community?* (London: The Federal Trust). A short book taking a generally pessimistic view of the economic, administrative and political consequences of Community expansion.

Warren, K. (1976), *The Geography of British Heavy Industry since 1800* (London: Oxford University Press). An industrial geography particularly relevant to the understanding of the present-day problems of traditional industrial regions.

Williamson, J. G. (1965), 'Regional inequality and the process of national development: a description of the patterns', *Economic Development and Cultural Change*, vol. 13, pp. 3–45. Reprinted in *Regional Analysis*, ed. L. Needleman (Harmondsworth: Penguin, 1968), pp. 99–158.

Williamson, J. (1975), 'The implications of European monetary integration for peripheral areas', in *Economic Sovereignty and Regional Policy*, ed. J. Vaizey (Dublin: Gill & Macmillan), pp. 105–21.

Wullkopf, V., and Pearce, A. E. (1977), 'Some views on long term trends in urban and regional research in Western Europe', *Urban Studies*, vol. 14, pp. 41–50.

Yannopoulos, G. N. (1977), 'The Mediterranean policy of the EEC', *Journal of World Trade Law*, vol. 11, pp. 489–500.

Yuill, D., Allen, K., and Hull, C. (1980), *Regional Policy in the European Community: The Role of Regional Incentives* (London: Croom Helm). A set of detailed national surveys, supported by a substantial conclusion.

Index

Printed in the United States
by Baker & Taylor Publisher Services